Fields of Connection

The practice of business constellations

Fields of Connection – *The practice of business constellations*

Jan Jacob Stam

Editing: James G. Campbell

Translation by: James G. Campbell

Originally published under title: Het verbindende veld

© 2017, Systemic Books Publishing

ISBN 978-9492331090 (NUR 801)

Contents

Acknowledgements

First of all I need to thank some people. Actually, that's not completely true. I do not want to thank them, I want to mention them. Thanking them is a process of acknowledging what I got from them. As live examples and role models for me they gave me their ideas and insights, and I cannot give them much back, besides being grateful. And thanking them is something between them and me, and the reader doesn't have anything to do with this rather intimate process of wanting to thank them.

You might even feel a little bit as though you are watching a peep-show when I thank the people from whom I got so much. No, I want to mention them, to let you know, and shout to the world, that these are people who made important and decisive contributions to the development of business constellations. Without these caring, dedicated, professional people, the whole systemic approach of business constellations would not exist, nor would this book.

So please, a warm round of applause for:

- Gunthard Weber, who took on the idea of doing organization constellations in the first place as a godfather and who has created a solid and broad base for their further development.

- Matthias Varga von Kibéd and Insa Sparrer, with their endless stream of fresh ideas, their observations, both acknowledging and supportive, that inspired one like a warm bubble bath.

- Bert Hellinger, for making constellation work possible at all, sharing all his insights without wanting anything back for it, like a fresh mountain spring, always available and from which all may drink their fill.

For a long time I was hesitant and reluctant about having this book translated into English. It would be better just to re-write the whole book; as it was written it is too Dutch; I felt it would need to be more solid in English whereas I had allowed myself a certain lightness in the Dutch version. The only way we could have this book translated into English was to have it be far from perfect. I do hope, you as a reader can live with that.

Robin Temple and Hendrikus Schumacher translated this book into English. For a control-freak like myself, I felt grateful that I could trust my product into their hands without reservations.

And I agree with the advertisement which states that the man behind an achievement is often a woman: my wife Bibi, who knows me so well and had to deal with all the doubts, bad temper and last minute work.

Jan Jacob Stam
Groningen, august 2006

Foreword

This book is designed to offer a short guided tour through the worlds of work and organisations, from a 'systemic' point of view. As we live our individual lives, surrounded by all the myriad possibilities and limitations that confront us each day, we can so easily forget that we are also intimately connected to the larger whole. The 'systemic' way of thinking and looking at the world helps us become aware of the many mechanisms and dynamics that are at work in systems that we normally never notice. These are the dynamics that can, in one moment, give us the wings to fly and in another moment hold us completely paralysed and unable to act. The German philosopher and psychotherapist Bert Hellinger has discovered a way to make the hidden dynamics of any system visible. He uses what he calls the 'constellation' to do this. Gunthard Weber, together with many colleagues, has developed Bert Hellinger's pioneering ideas further and taken constellations into the world of work and professions and organisations. A 'constellation' has the unique capacity of being able to bring fundamental truths about any particular system to light. It bypasses the opinions or judgements that so we easily impose on reality and which tend to filter out and distort the truth. And, as such, the constellation approach is very directly connected with perceivable reality.

Constellations have been able to provide us with many new insights into how organisations actually function and how people within organisations can flourish. The interest in organisational constellations is naturally growing very rapidly now with so much new information becoming available about what is actually going on in organisations, when considered from a systemic point of view.

I, myself, through my work as an organisational consultant, have now had six years of experience using the systemic approach in organisations. I've brought many insights together in this book, examples from our consulting practice, and my own experiences gained from working in the field of organisation constellations.

The material in this book is presented as a series of articles, arranged in no particular sequence. So I invite you to choose for yourself the order in which you read them.

If you are someone for whom the methods of organisation or system constellations are new you, might want to start with Chapter 7. How about a conducted tour? Perhaps, by wandering through the landscape of our working lives, with this book in your hand, your attention will be drawn to a few special places of interest. I wish you a pleasant walk as you explore!

Jan Jacob Stam
Abries, France, october 2003

The system we call 'the organisation'

1

1.1 A systemic 'quick reference' card

Perhaps a couple of years from now you could be someone who is arriving at your first day in a new job in a organisation you will be working for. Alongside the standard issue of your I.D. card with PIN code, map of the building, org. chart and list of abbreviations used in this organisation, you are also handed a systemic quick-reference card. On this card you would be able to see, at a glance, all the most important systemic dynamics that are operating within the company for whom you are about to start working. These systemic dynamics are the invisible winds that blow through this company. These unseen winds have the power to give people wings to fly. Equally, against their wishes and without their being aware of it, these unseen forces can actually make people ill. The 'orgenogram' is a sort of org. chart of the history of the company. By looking at this chart, together with the systemic quick-reference card that you have been given, you would be able to get a much clearer picture for yourself of the place where you are about to start working and where you hope to remain happily working for the foreseeable future.

On the systemic quick-reference card the following dynamics of the company might be indicated:

The founder of this company was a man of ideals who wanted to help many people in a poor neighbourhood and decided to set up a co-operative venture to do this. After working in this company for many years he finally left to set up a new company.

Many of the present employees still remain more loyal to the original founder of their company than to the present board of directors.

Many years ago the company changed from being a cooperative to being a limited company and entered new market sectors. One member of the present board of directors still identifies himself with the original market sector that the company was working in, even though the company no longer operates in this sector. His fellow board members often experience him as a bit of a 'pain in the ass', although some employees actually do like him very much.

In the management of the technical department a few black marks on the reference card indicate some areas are under pressure here: whatever they do manage to achieve in this particular department never seems to be enough and the illness ratio amongst them is pretty high.

After a re-organisation in the company six years ago several managers found themselves placed in positions that did not exist systemically within the organisation and ended up being put in charge of a department that was not really necessary for the continuation of the system (one of these managers is presently applying for a new job at the moment).

The company as a whole has a lively balance in give and take with the provincial town where they are located: some local festivals are sponsored by the company and each year one of the company's production facilities is offered as the departure point of an ice-skating event. The city is proud to have this company located in their city and the company itself is openly proud to be rooted in this area. Two of the five production teams have had, for many years now, a good atmosphere and a high problem-solving capability.

This is the case despite the fact that employees and team leaders in these teams have had to submit themselves to frequent job rotations. We wish you a pleasant stay, a satisfying and increasing balance between give and take and we offer you a place that is right for you where you can excel.

1.2 An organisation

What is an organisation, really, from the systemic-thinking point of view that was first developed by the German philosopher and psycho-therapist Bert Hellinger in the context of family systems?

An organisation can have existed for hundreds of years. There will be no-one left who was there when it was founded and yet the organisation has remained essentially the same. An employee is connected for a certain time with an organisation, contributes to the development of that organisation, goes through personal development him- or herself, and then leaves. The place in the organisation that had been occupied by that person becomes available and someone else takes over that position for a while.

In an organisation people function as representatives in a system constellation. They take up a position. There are systemic dynamics operating on this position and also the personal dynamics brought in by the person who is presently occupying that position.

Then that person leaves, while the position in the organisation's system remains. The position gives a certain 'bandwidth' of freedom of movement to whomever occupies that position. Such a position carries with it both possibilities and restrictions, all embedded within the larger whole.

From this point of view is an organisation perhaps less malleable than we think or would prefer to have it be?

1.3 What makes an organisation healthy?

What conditions are necessary for an organisation to be healthy? 'Health' here means that the employees in that organisation feel good and are able to work effectively. It also implies that the organisation fulfils the purposes in society for which it was originally established and that there is lively exchange within the organisation itself and between the organisation and the 'outside world'. In short a healthy organisation is somewhere where you really would want to be working.

As a system an organisation has many parts: the workers, the customers , the products and services provided by the organisation, the mission or objectives of the organisation and many other elements. The system as a whole has qualities different from just the sum of its parts and can be seen, in this way, to be very much the same as a living organism. In the same way a whole human being possesses qualities that are more than just the sum of all of his or her organs put together.

The system of an organisation demonstrates its own set of dynamics. These dynamics are separate from the people who are part of that system in any moment.

When we talk of 'dynamics' we are talking about what is going on between the various elements in a system and the relationships those elements have with each other.

These dynamics directly influence the behaviours and feelings of those people within the system. Unfortunately system dynamics are not directly perceivable and they work beyond the conscious domain of our everyday awareness.

The effects of system dynamics are noticeable enough though! Positive effects will be experienced by people and described in such expressions as: *"I am in the right place here." "We are working in an energetic organisation that is full of life." "We can respond to changes appropriately, are good at decision-making and have good contact with the outside world."*

The negative effects of system dynamics will be experienced as problems within an organisation: *"It's not working." "We have internal communication problems." "It's like it is not allowed to work out." "We are not as skilled here as we know we are capable of being"*, and so on. Actually these expressions of the problem are not the actual problem, but descriptions of the reactions of the system to specific system dynamics. Knowing this we can look at the presenting difficulties through different eyes: We can ask ourselves, for example: *"What is happening here in the background in this system, that causes people to experience there being a problem?"*.

A system can function healthily if it takes the following basic principles into account:

1. Everyone has equal right to a place within the system

2. There is a correct order of positions within any system

3. In any exchange there needs to be a balance between give and take

In a healthy organisation all the people working in that organisation are seen for who they are. This is true not only for those people presently working in the organisation but also for anyone who, historically speaking, has some sort of significance for the organisation.

Obviously the significant people in the history of an organisation would include the founders of the organisation, but also anyone in the past who made a noticeable contribution to the growth or survival of the system as a whole. In a healthy organisation such people are respected.

In the consciousness of the system itself these people have their own place within the system, without the organisation having to be dependent on them. Any healthy organisation will be directed towards the future but will have the founders present in the background as a source of supporting strength.

For the employees in a healthy organisation it holds true that: irrespective of the function a person has within the system, whether it be a manager or a store-house operative, every person has his or her own rightful place within the system and is seen and valued equally. They will all be different but will be valued equally.

You will find in any healthy organisation that there is a particular arrangement of positions within the system of that organisation. This order or arrangement has to do with the purposes of the organisation. The person whose job it is to create the structure within which all the other people function will come in first position in the system. The person who creates the structure for those who follow will occupy the second place and so on. In this way everybody has his own position, which he can trust and from where he can do his job well.

Finally there is the balance of give and take. Everyone in an organisation contributes to that organisation through the job he or she is doing and receives something back from the organisation in a constant exchange of back and forth that can also increase over time. This is not only true for the employees of an organisation but also for the organisation as a whole. There will be a constant exchange between the organisation and its customers, suppliers and others.

When the organisation is healthy this interchange can be continuously growing and expanding and changing, depending on the movement of the organisation itself. Growth can be measured in terms of amount, but also in intensity or quality. For this reason long-established organisations are important. They are important not because they are somehow 'important', as such, but because they will be connected to many, many people and their families and many people will have given their best to such an organisation, sometimes for many years. A head of such an organisation will also, thus, have much importance too. Such an organisation will also attract what is new and the leaders of such an organisation will need to decide what does and what does not work and what is the best moment to take on something new. In this way also it can happen that an organisation comes to a point in its life when its time is up. At that moment it is much the best thing if the organisation chooses to stop, dissolve itself and make room for something new to appear in its place.

Bert Hellinger noticed a particular power at work in systems. A power that works to preserve the continuity of the system itself. He called this power the 'collective conscience'. Here again we have the idea that the whole is more than, and works differently than, the sum of the parts. The collective conscience tries to repair any dents and scratches that the system receives. Sometimes parts of the system are readily sacrificed in order to preserve the whole, just as a lizard, to save its own life, will release its tail when attacked. The collective conscience mostly works unconsciously, rather than through conscious decisions. In its attempts to recover from particularly major or traumatic incidents during its lifetime, any long-standing organisation may grow crooked and end up with all sorts of scars on it that add something very special and unique to the character of such an organisation.

The healing powers of any system and the dynamics associated with systems will be brought into play in any circumstance where the underlying conditions needed for a system to be healthy (mentioned above) are not being met.

The collective conscience of a system is not interested in the reasons why something is happening. It simply reacts to facts and events.

The system of an organisation will not allow someone or something that is essential to that organisation to be excluded. If, for example, a manager is dismissed in an inappropriate way, or is not acknowledged by his or her successor, or is spoken about in a condescending way, it is as if the place of that manager in the system is being denied. The result of this denial will be that, at some point later, someone will behave in a way that corresponds to the feelings of the manager who was not properly given his place in the system. Just like that manager the person reflecting that manager's situation might have the feeling he needs to leave the organisation or, in another way, would want to bring that forgotten manager back into the picture.

If a product, that previously has made a name for a particular company, is set aside at some point inappropriately, then other products from that company will fail. There is nothing moralistic in all of this. It is just what has been observed happening over and over again. From the systemic point of view whatever comes first has to have a position above what comes later. If what came first is respected as such then what comes later will take up a good position in the system. Then there will also be room for something new to happen. This means that those who come into an organisation later should not interfere in the affairs of those who were there first. In organisations it works in the form of a hierarchy.

A management team that feels itself to be superior to the board of directors will, in the end, not be able to function effectively. With the help of system constellations we can see that the collective conscience will always try to repair what is damaged within the system. This repair will have to happen at the cost of those who come into the organisation after the damage has been done. That is why we see so many 'second-generation' issues in organisations. Unconsciously, the second-generation has been hired to repair what has been damaged before they arrive or to represent someone in the organisation who has been excluded at some point. Again here we are not looking at any value judgements about anyone. Someone who might feel him or herself to be better than the management is often doing this in an attempt to do something good for whatever it is that is cherished by him or her. This is experienced as 'rebellion out of love'. But, since the rebellion inevitably brings this person into a position in the system where he or she does not belong, these attempts to put something to rights inevitably fail. The system itself will not allow the order of the system to be disturbed. Managers often find rebellions difficult to handle. You cannot put rebellions into any sort of order and it feels sometimes as if your position is not being respected at all. But deep down you can always ask yourself: *"What is so precious for this particular person that she or he is willing make it into an issue and so to run the risk to be kicked out of the organisation?"* When you listen carefully to what a rebel has to say you often get important information about the system as a whole. And in that sense rebels can be important sources of (systemic) information.

Whenever there is an outstanding debt the system will intervene. When, for example, a company has become rich at the cost of other people's health and welfare, then that company will have incurred a debt to those people.

At a later date there will have to be people within that company's system who take on the burden of this old debt or try to do penance for what has happened in the past in an attempt to restore the balance between give and take demanded by the system. These people will do this without knowing anything at all about this debt. They will also not be consciously wanting to do anything about this debt. They will sometimes even unconsciously pay with their own health and welfare and in this way join sides with the past victims of the company.

Dynamics

2

In this chapter we will review a number of these recognisable dynamics that arise whenever a system attempts to restore balance. We will present a number of real-life examples drawn from our practice. This chapter is about the dynamics of the organisation's system itself. We will consider what we can bring from our own family systems into organisations in an other chapter.

2.1 Triangulation

Anja works as a coach, coaching an employee of a company. After the session, which is happening in the company's offices, the boss of the employee casually asks her if she doesn't mind coming into his office for a little chat. Although Anja feels a little uneasy about this request she lets herself be drawn into a conversation. The boss asks her how it is going with that particular employee and if he is progressing, because, well, you know, he is worried about that employee. Anja answers his questions but on the way home she feels bad about what happened. How come she let herself be lured into answering these questions from this boss?

The code for the coaching bureau for whom she works is to not divulge to the employer any information regarding the content of sessions with clients during a coaching course. This had clearly been agreed upon beforehand. Here, again, she finds herself in the middle of a conflict between two other people. A conflict in which she should not be involved and in which she especially does not want to be involved. This situation seems to happen repeatedly to her: she is pulled in two directions by conflicting loyalties while, in fact, she should be completely uninvolved. This dynamic is called 'triangulation'.

Triangulation is a disturbance in the order of a system. Someone has arrived at a higher level in the hierarchy than is his or her rightful place. This usually happens in conflict situations and the person affected ends up in between the two or more parties involved in the conflict. In daily life a person will experience this in the role of being a mediator. The position of mediator is tempting because of the status it offers. But one can very quickly fall into being presumptuous in such a position and thereby can end up being mistrusted by others.

Very often in training situations I've let slip a remark to someone such as: *"I feel you might be in the wrong position. You should be in the management team"*. Often such an incidental remark has the effect of purifying something for the person hearing it said. Employees have no real business with what is going on at the level of their direct managers. Conflicts should always remain at the appropriate level within any hierarchy. When employees get involved in conflicts it is an open invitation to become trapped.

A woman, head of the accounting department of a railway company in Croatia, told me she did not know anymore to whom she should report. Her manager was in a power struggle with another person who aspired to be in this position. In a constellation these two men stood close together and the tension between them and in the surrounding space was high. When I asked this woman how she could possibly report the quarterly accounts in this situation she suddenly started to laugh. She took a piece of paper, tore it in half and offered both the men a 'report'. Immediately both men turned towards her and she was in danger of being drawn into their conflict. Shocked by how recognisable this situation was to her she tried another way. She took one report and laid it respectfully at their feet. Both men accepted this gesture with a nod and went on with their conflict. The woman sighed with relief and went on with her work, without being drawn into the conflict and without any judgement about who rightfully should hold the position of manager.

Triangulation looks very much like being 'seduced'. Someone from the management team asks for your opinion about some problem going on there. It starts off so apparently innocently. You feel a little flattered being consulted, especially when you feel your opinion is valued. But, at a certain point, the feeling starts to creep in: *"What have I got myself involved in here? I'm not sure I want to know more about all of this"*. It starts to feel inappropriate but then it is not so easy to withdraw. Slowly you find yourself becoming involved in something in which, strictly speaking, you do not belong. When triangulation is at work you can recognise it by the embarrassing fact that the more you know about what is going on at a higher level in the hierarchy the more the managers are weakened rather than strengthened. At first it may seem that such a peek into the intimate world of the managers makes them all the more human, but it actually weakens their position. If you are not careful you are faced with an invitation to become more involved. This is especially true for anyone who is already connected with situations in which triangulation is at work. These are people who, from having triangulation present in the system of their own family, are thus more sensitive to this dynamic in general.

Triangulation can be stopped. It is possible for an employee to disentangle himself or herself from such a situation by saying something like: *"I am just an employee."* The manager says: *"You are an employee. I am your boss and next to me are my colleagues. We can handle what is going on between us. Stay out of it".* These sentences, of course, need not be spoken out loud. It is more a matter of attitude and of taking a different position in the situation that is presenting itself. Any person can go back, internally, to his or her position within the hierarchy and the others in the system will also notice this unconsciously. This disentangling movement can be performed in many different ways and it returns everyone involved to his or her dignity, position and power.

2.2 Parentification: reversing the order

" *Nobody can beat the boss.* "

Bert Hellinger

"In fact I feel better than the boss, I am actually above him. Well, actually, now you come to mention it, I feel better than the whole board of directors. Deep in my heart I despise them a bit for the way they are managing this company that is so close to my heart. I would do it differently if I were in charge. Do you want to hear how?"

Parentification in organisations leads to anxiety and loss of energy. The attention of the employees goes more into holding their positions than into the work itself. Anyone who steps into an organisation and who listens and watches for a while can quickly get an impression of whether this dynamic is powerfully at work or not.

A specialist in a department may feel more competent than his boss. When it is about the content of what he is doing, this may very well be the case.

But there is a danger if he starts to feel superior and to feel he is of more value than his manager in the area of management. If this is the attitude of the specialist there will inevitably be problems. When looking for a solution to such a problem order must be restored to the system. The boss would say to the employee: *"You are good at your trade and I value for that"*. If this is said in a benign way, the employee can say: *"You are my boss and you can use me as your employee"*. Again these sentences only reflect a shift in attitude and position in the system and need not necessarily be said out loud. In a large energy company the in-house organisation consultants were in constant conflict with their manager. The consultants had a lot of complaints about their manager. They thought he was not managing their section well and simple necessities, like management of the department's schedule, were not being met. This manager also was not cultivating enough goodwill for them in the organisation as a whole.

The manager invited me to take the whole department to the country for a day and to come back with a relationship that worked. It became clear to me that most of the employees of this department felt themselves to be better than their manager. Their manager was kind, a somewhat timid man, but with enough proven management qualities. I chose to work in the following way: We all came together, including the manager, and everyone had a chance to speak. In this first round every employee could say what he or she needed to have to be able to do good work. The formulation of the question was critical. As soon as one of the employees began to say what the manager should be doing differently or to complain about what was wrong with the organisation, he or she was brought back to the question: *"What is needed to allow you to do your job well?"*. Proceeding in this way every employee in the department was able to say what was needed. Nobody was allowed to react to what was being said, everyone listened, including the manager.

After this first round a second round was begun with the question: *"Having heard everything from the first round, what do you think would be good proposals for this department?"*. Anyone who wanted to say something in this second round was able to do so. The manager just listened and there was no discussion. Then the manager had a chance to speak. He could speak right away or leave it a week. He said what proposals he would adopt and which not. What was remarkable during this meeting, which lasted an afternoon, was that everything became quieter and quieter. And with this growing stillness the things people were saying also carried more weight.

When a person speaks about what he or she needs in order to do his or her job well this declaration is connected to 'primary' emotions, which, in turn, are directly connected to reality. In the moment of expressing those needs a person is taking full responsibility for his or her job and is serious about this job. If someone complains about the boss or organisation this will usually be done with a great deal of noise but there will be little force behind it. Complaining is always connected to 'secondary' feelings, which cover up the underlying primary needs of a person. The meeting produced many useful proposals, supported by many of the group. But, apart from that obvious benefit, most importantly, it was a systemic intervention. By asking the question *"What do you need to do your job well?"*, the consultants were invited to re-possess their own positions within the system and not to take up a position above that of the manager.

2.3 Identification with a goal

"On the one hand I'm inspired and it's enjoyable and challenging work. On the other hand I find, again and again, I'm losing myself. I sometimes can't see any more what I'm doing all of this for.
I don't know when to stop and I would like to exchange some of my perfectionism for a bit more of being able to take it easy."

A project manager had difficulties finishing off his project. On reflection it became clear that the he could not get his colleagues to adopt the outcome of the project, although many of them actually wanted such an outcome. We started the constellation having first set up a representative for the project manager himself and a representative for the colleagues who would benefit from the outcome of the project. In the constellation the project manager came across as being arrogant. This was strange as it was not the way he presented himself within the company. Then it became clear that his colleagues were not actually seeing the project manager when they looked at him but were looking at something else – the goal of the project.

When the project manager and the goal of the project were separated, by lacing two different representatives in the constellation, one for the goal and one for the project manager himself, the project manager became human again in the eyes of his co-workers, and was acceptable as a colleague. Seeing him in this way they could work together with him. The project manager, for his part, realised that, unknowingly, he had slowly become more and more overwhelmed by the goal of the project and this had also, personally, taken a great toll on him. It quite frequently happens that someone will get identified with a goal or an assignment. Then you no longer have a goal but the goal has you. When your colleagues start jokingly referring to you as: *"Hey, here comes Miss Sustainable Building"* it's time for you to start wondering what might be going on and if this is actually what you want to be happening. Often the goal actually belongs somewhere else - to management or the board of directors. If these people cannot make a decision about the goal it will look for someone else to attach itself to so that it can make sure it is not forgotten.

But because it is not your goal (of course it is basically yours, because it is such a wonderful goal!) it ends up that you find yourself carrying something that actually belongs to someone else. This is when it starts to become a burden. This is because when you start carrying someone else's goal, however beautiful it may be, it ends up being an endless prayer. The goal becomes weakened when this happens; you become weaker too, and eventually even the person who originally had the goal becomes weakened.

2.4 Facing something that someone else cannot see

Twenty years ago Rolf and his wife set up a school for difficult adolescents in Stockholm. In fact, what happened was that a number of adolescents asked them to do that. Today Rolf is struggling with his position as principal of the school. In a constellation the employees of the school were showing signs of being afraid. When I asked them if they felt it was that their jobs were at stake, Rolf denied that this was the case. Then it became clear that the employees were being afraid of something else and were acting as if they were afraid of being punished or of being judged, but not by Rolf or his wife. Rolf 's representative in this constellation looked quite powerless in the situation. We then placed a representative for 'the judgmental entity' (without knowing exactly what this element stood for, but the representatives behaved as if they felt afraid being judged). This changed everything. The representative for Rolf 's wife suddenly became very powerful, 'Rolf' came to life and the 'employees' relaxed. The real Rolf, who was sitting next to me, looking very intently at the constellation, then said *"This is the judiciary, who are empowered to take children from their homes and bring them to us"*. When Rolf had started the school: young, idealistic and incensed by what was wrong in society, he had turned his back on the judicial authorities. What he was not able to see his employees were able to see for him.

They also had taken over a fear that was not theirs and which belonged, in fact, to Rolf himself.

2.5 We try to solve something that is not solved at another level

Very often we also see a whole team being taken over by something that has remained unsolved at another level in the system of an organisation. When this happens there will be recurring conflicts happening in the team. Team members will be looking for solutions, voicing their opinions, making agreements and yet, again and again, things return to being strained.

When this sort of situation is happening you might start wondering if the team is, in fact, trying to solve a problem that remains unsolved at a higher level. At a university a wide-ranging program of change was being planned. The plan was focussed around becoming more market-oriented and commercial, by developing contract work; the faculties had to make their expertise available to local enterprises at a price equivalent to the going-rate for such contract work in the market. The team of four directors responsible for this program of change were wondering if they should introduce the proposed changes throughout the whole organisation in the same uniform way, or have each department in the organisation choose their own course of change. They needed a decision fast because there were signs of unrest amongst the middle-managers and employees. Everything was taking much too long, a new facility being built was just about to come on-line and so everything needed to be done as quickly as possible.We had a meeting with these four directors: the general manager and the three other directors. The head of the technology department wanted to do a constellation with his management team because there was a lot of tension amongst his colleagues. The board of directors was set up as a constellation along with the technology department's team.

To everyone's astonishment both teams showed exactly the same patterns and the representatives in both teams felt exactly the same as each other. The technology department's team was trying to solve a problem that lay with the board of directors. It became clear that the tension in the technology department's team was tension that had been taken over from the tension amongst the board of directors. The pattern of relationships seen in the board of directors had been completely replicated at the lower-level in the system of the technology department's management team. In such a situation the solution would not be found in the technology department's team. They could go off together somewhere in the country for another three sessions and make all sorts of agreements together. But if the source of the tension is not in their own team then nothing would be resolved by doing that.

2.6 I'll follow you

The following example will illustrate how 'second-generation' problems can arise in organisations.

An energetic and successful consultancy company wanted to do a day about organisation constellations for all the members of the company. They also wanted to bring in a question about their own company and did this at the end of the day. It was the group of junior employees who most felt the need to bring in an issue. They had discussed it previously and the theme of their question had to do with the structure of the company itself. They felt responsible for the structure of the company and at the same time uneasy about it. We did a constellation in which three 'generations' were represented. Firstly there were the founders of the company that had left the company some years previously and moved on to do other things. Secondly the present management and board, successors of the founders, were set up in the constellation.

And thirdly the junior employees, who had only been with the company a couple of years, were set up. In the constellation a number of the representatives for the junior employees felt the inclination to leave the system. The real employees spoke, with pain in their hearts, about how they did actually feel this inclination to leave. Their representatives in the constellation were constantly wanting to look towards the representatives of the founders in the constellation. Only when the founders reassured the junior employees that they, themselves, were doing fine, and that they had handed over the management of the company to the present management team, could the junior employees allow themselves to relax a little. The junior employees were touched when the founders said to them: "*You can preserve our principles and if you use them well we'll be really pleased*". They were especially moved by the way the representatives of the junior employees and the founders were looking at each other in the constellation.

It is truly strange how second generation employees can feel so connected to the founders of an organisation, none of whom they have ever met or known, and feel so concerned about the destiny of the founders themselves, and the legacy they have been given charge of by the founders. This seems to be much less so in the case with the first generation of successors of the founders of a company who take over and continue with a company.

We see this very often in constellations. If you notice there is restlessness in the sense of "*Should I stay or should I leave?*", or if there is a considerable turnover in staff, without any obvious cause, it pays to consider who in the past has left this organisation?

2.7 Non-existent positions

In 1998 I had just come across the systemic-phenomenological point of view when a housing co-operative asked me, as an organisation consultant, to look at a problem in their organisation. At that time I had no idea that this approach would uncover such a wealth of insights into just how organisations work or do not work.

The 'problem' this cooperative had, appeared to be a manager, one of the three members of the board of directors. He was a nice man, educated, energetic and with excellent management qualities. According to his employees, three department heads, and quite a few of his colleagues, he was causing 'tears' in the organisation. One employee was already staying at home, there had been lots of meetings in which many of the tensions within the organisation had been talked about, but to no avail. The strange thing was that nobody could quite put their finger on the sore spot in the organisation. One of the department heads said, remarkably: *"His presence causes a kind of paralysis. We sit there and look at it and for whatever reason we simply don't seem to know how to get ourselves out of it"*.

Nowadays I know that these symptoms are a clue to the fact that somewhere there is a 'stuckness' in the system. Then, back in 1998, I was at my wit's end as to what to do since I, also, had no idea what could be going on. In the end, with some trepidation because it was all so new, we set up a constellation. Something remarkable happened. The position for the third manager was not available in the system. That night the general manager called me and said: *"It fits. Originally there were just the two directors, the technical manager and myself. The man who is now creating all the problems was hired by us to be a project manager. He was so good at what he was doing that we wanted to keep him.*

So we made him internal affairs director, with everyone's full support. But, it really makes sense, we never really created that third place on the board of directors. For the project manager himself it was painful because he had been feeling for the past three years that something was wrong, had worked really hard to get it right and now realised that he had never had a chance from the very beginning. But it was also a relief for him. A relief to know that it was not just him. His battered self-confidence had come from his position within the system of the organisation where he had been tied down. Being in this position his possibilities had been severely restricted".

It's very much a new idea that there is the possibility for there to be a non-existent position within an organisation. You are appointed to do a particular function, are you not? But many organisation constellations have painfully revealed the reality of this phenomenon. With new functions it is especially important to first create the position within the system before someone is taken on to fill that position. Here is another example from a local council organisation.

2.8 The council clerk

In the process of dividing up of responsibilities within the local government authorities, where a distinction has been made between the managers of the local authorities and the members of the local council who represent the local population, a new function has been created: the council clerk. The council clerk is an official secretary and he supports the local city council. Before the council clerk existed this function was performed as part of the duties of the town clerk. The town clerk is manager of the local authority organisation and secretary to the board of the mayor and town councillors.

In earlier days the town clerk was also then secretary to the town council. In a short workshop done with seven new council clerks the following issue was brought in by Peter, a participant. Peter: *"I've been a council clerk now for ten months and my position is still unclear. I don't worry about it every day but it is an important issue for me to be resolved"*. Without much additional information Peter set up representatives for: the mayor, two party spokesmen (A and B), the town clerk and the council clerk. The mayor and the two party spokespersons were positioned in a triangle. At some distance away was the town clerk and behind him was the council clerk.

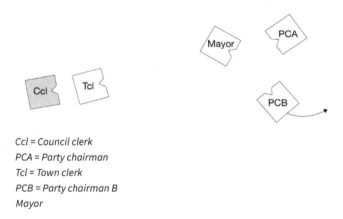

Ccl = Council clerk
PCA = Party chairman
Tcl = Town clerk
PCB = Party chairman B
Mayor

The participants noticed right away that there seemed to be two sub-systems within the constellation: The mayor with the two party chairmen formed one sub-system and the town clerk and the council clerk formed another. Party Chairman B wanted to see the town clerk and so turned in their direction. The mayor was feeling good in the position he was in. Party Chairman A was feeling strong and from his attitude and responses it was clear that he was in charge of the system as a whole. Peter confirmed this.

The constellation showed that the position of the council clerk was difficult to fill. As soon as the representatives for the town clerk and the council clerk were placed opposite each other it was clear that something was going on between them both.

Then I asked myself, as the facilitator in this constellation, *"Who appointed the council clerk?"* Everyone hesitated to answer. Perhaps the council? So I asked: *"Who conducts the performance interviews?"* Participants: *"No-one really."* One of the participants eventually says: *"I have the party chairmen do them".*

In the proposed system the mayor did not project much of a directing force in the whole situation. It was the Party Chairman A who has this sort of presence. He said: *"I do feel connected to the town clerk. But I don't feel any connection yet with the council clerk".* He then said to the town clerk: *"A part of your work has been taken away from you. This has nothing to do with you as a person".* The council clerk then replied: *"You have been here a long time, as town clerk of the council. I do realise this and respect it. I will take over this work now, in my new role."* It felt really good for both the town clerk and the council clerk that this had been said.

Then we looked for a final depiction of the system, where all the representatives would feel in their right places.

Both the council clerk and the party chairmen felt it best if the council clerk stood to the left of the party chairmen. Systemically this means that the council clerk is supporting the role of the chairmen and the council.

In the following joint discussion with all seven council workers a number of provisional conclusions were drawn: In this a constellation the town clerk and council clerk define their positions with each other. The town clerk is valued for the work he did as secretary for the council. It was acknowledged that this function had now come to an end and the party chairman would now take on this function. This process of ending a function and handing over to someone else had not taken place in the organisations in which the participants in this workshop were working. For this function to really succeed it would seem to require that there would be either some body or person, higher up in the system than the town clerk and the council clerk, that came into place. This was needed to bring the previous role of the secretary to a satisfactory end and to really create a new place for the council clerk to work in. It could work out well if this process of ending such a long-standing function were to be achieved with some form of small ceremony. Peter said in this concluding conversation that his situation at work was not really tolerable any more and if things didn't change soon he would start to think about leaving.

All seven of the council clerks present at this workshop had previously been working in the civil service organization of the local government. Five of them mentioned that their loyalty was more with this civil service organisation and two of them felt that their loyalties lay more with the political organization of the city-council. Some of the five who felt more loyal to the civil service organisation commented that they were this way out of some kind of need for a feeling of security. If they were to fail in their function in any way they would still be accepted back into the civil service organisation.

A number of them also cautiously mentioned that they felt they were betraying their fellow civil servants when they fully identified with and were loyal to the political part of the system, the city council. Two council clerks still had two more years of service before they were entitled to take up the early retirement scheme offered by the council. They were both remarkably energetic and creating the new function and one of them commented: *"I am free, no-one can interfere with me"*.

A new function cannot simply be brought into existence by saying to someone: *"I hereby appoint you to this new function"*. The function, and the person who is going to fill that function, are two different factors in a system. Only after a function has been properly installed can people begin to successfully fill that function. If someone leaves the function then becomes available for someone else to fill it. From experience we've learnt that in creating a new function a great deal of authority is required from a person situated one or two management levels above that at which the new function is being created. A new function has to be fitted into the system correctly and there needs to be someone who creates the framework or structure within which this new function can have every chance of succeeding. This new function, in its turn, creates the framework within which others can function correctly. In this way the function also contributes to the functioning of the organisation as a whole.

Sometimes a manager will appoint an assistant because he is too busy to do all the parts of his function himself. If the function of the assistant so hired is not clear then you can see such a function turning into a 'non-function'. The position of assistant manager does not really exist, as itself, within the system. Many assistant managers have found themselves feeling quite unhappy in such positions, as being just some sort of extra capacity for the manager.

2.9 Positions that are 'burdened'

Sometimes in organisations you will find positions that just have too much of a burden placed on them. This can be found in single positions within an organisation or within a whole department. Whoever takes on a function that has this quality of being burdened will experience the function as being one that, in some way, is either not allowed to succeed or not allowed to exist for very long. You might find, for example, that in a particular management function four people have left that position in the last three years. They start off in the function all full of energy, but end up having to leave after a while, just to protect themselves. Or, for example, in a restaurant, one after another the cooks come and then leave again shortly thereafter, without there being any apparent cause for such a high turnover of staff. A position in a system may take on this quality of being 'burdened' if, for example, a person filling that position in an organisation left the function under negative circumstances. This might have been because of an unresolved conflict, an accident, or a person who has died or been somehow excluded from the system of the organisation.

Here is an example of how a whole department of an organisation was burdened by something. A young woman psychologist was working for a year in a psycho-geriatric care organisation.

She described the theme of the issue that she wanted to bring into a constellation as 'a trauma in the organisation'. This issue seemed to repeat itself over and over again within her organisation – influencing the whole atmosphere there and preventing cooperation between employees in the organisation. She described how, years before she arrived to take up her function within the organisation, some residents of the care organisation had been abused and the offenders had subsequently been fired.

Set up in the constellation were: a representative for the victims and, some time later, a representative for the offenders. The representative for the offenders could not look the representative for the victims in the eye. The offender looked down at the floor and appeared to be uneasy. He said he felt uncomfortable, feels hot and his hands are sweating. The victim said to the offender: *"Please look at me!"* Eventually, after a long pause, the offender looked up at the victim and they looked at each other for a long time. Then representatives for the board of directors of the institution and the department head were set up in the constellation. Neither of these two were able to look directly at either the victims or the offenders. The representative for the psychologist who had brought up the issue then began shaking uncontrollably. She only could start to relax again a little when she looked at the victims for a long time.

At this moment we stopped the constellation. Both the participants in the constellation itself and those in the group observing the constellation were very moved by what had happened. The representative of the victims confessed that the thing that was actually far worse than the abuse itself was the fact that the victims' simple human dignity had not been seen and acknowledged. They had the feeling they were no longer being seen as human beings but merely as victims.

The offenders who had been fired from their positions also felt they were no longer seen as human beings and this had excluded them from the system. Only after both the victims and the offenders were included, as human beings, could a movement take place within the system as a whole that allowed all the participants to regain a sense of peace.

2.10 Acknowledging what is present

All the system dynamics and examples we have been describing here are a way of confirming that systems of organisations are extremely resilient. This is so even in situations where the dynamics themselves will be painful for the individuals within that system. The mechanisms of these systems operate at a level that is beyond judgements, ideologies or beliefs. They are simply there, usually hidden in the background. Knowing this it gives added meaning to the expression: 'being in service to'. Accepting a function in an organization is not only a matter of consenting to the particular job itself but consenting to the whole and the fate of the organization. There are many more connections and inter-connections within any particular organisation than meets the eye. When we make sure that we acknowledge that these connections do actually exist, and we begin to see how they operate within any organisation, we have something that is very useful. We have the chance to recognise what sort of conditions need to be present for any organisation, and the people who work within that organisation, to flourish and succeed.

A new economy:
Systemic money
and turnover

3

3.1 New values

While all the hype around the dot.com 'explosion' was going on I became more and more amazed by what my 18 yr.-old son was getting up to. He was (and still is) a Linux adept and Microsoft hater. One day he asked me, in an off-hand sort of way, where you had to go to register yourself as a business. I directed him to the local Chamber of Commerce. He wanted to build an index programme for the Linux operating system together with two of his friends. According to him he would need a more powerful computer to do this and in order to have this computer he wanted to start up a small business. I, of course, imagined he wanted to also make some money with this new business. But this was not his intention at all. When it comes to computer operating systems I'm always hopelessly out of touch with what the latest developments are. So I was happy for him to enlighten me in this and other related matters. From what I understand Linux is far more than just a simple operating system. It is a whole philosophy and way of life. It is what is known as an 'open' operating system. Anyone can download it from the Internet and if someone develops something new for the Linux system they are able to share this with everyone else. This is how everyone can participate in adding to the Linux system and how it keeps on growing. My son and his two friends had noticed that Linux did not have its own index search engine. This seemed to them to be something that would be a useful contribution to the Linux community.

At first they kept quiet about their plan because they didn't want other of their friends to steal their idea before they were ready to launch their new project. When I (stupidly) asked if they were expecting to get anything back from their investment my son replied: *"That'll happen one day, in its own time"*. Something really struck me in the way he had said this. He wasn't saying it out of a sort of naive child-like trust that he would be taken care of in some way. And it was also not said by someone who had no idea about how the world really works. Nor was he coming from some idealistic belief. It sounded to me like a new truth that my son had expressed in his own way. A new way that things work. A new economy, perhaps. Maybe even the real 'new economy', in which other balances, of give and take, are in charge rather than those we are all so used to – of prices and charges that operate in the present-day market place.

3.2 Getting the balance between give and take

For those of us who go to work every day there is one mechanism about which we are all very sensitive. This is the whole matter of getting the balance between give and take right. This dynamic is much more powerfully at play within our working environments than it is within the environment of our families. Perhaps that is why whenever someone enters to the world of work one of the first things that needs to be handled is this issue of give and take. For most people this is not something that you are aware of while you are being brought up.

We all have a sort of systemic 'sixth-sense' that is highly sensitive to the balance between give and take. This sixth-sense is what tells us in any moment if we owe something to someone or if they owe us.

Imagine for a moment that you've been given something by someone. Immediately you will start to feel a need or even pressure in you to give something back in return. If what you give in return is slightly more than what you have received then the other person, in turn, will feel obliged to give something back to you. If that, also, is a little more than you gave an ever-increasing exchange of give and take has been created. This dynamic will then be the basis on which an ever more rich interchange can take place. Such a continuously, slowly growing exchange is often felt in the form of having contact with other people and society that is full of life. Perhaps we have an organisation that is held together by such an exchange of give and take. It forms the foundation for harmonious labour relations and is obviously an exchange not just in monetary terms but can take on many forms and guises. Someone does some work and, in return, receives many different things: job and financial security, reassurance that that person's family will be fed and will be able to go off on holiday, a place in which to belong, a social life, a salary etc. etc.

This balancing mechanism seems to work very precisely. It also does not always match what has been negotiated within any particular situation. For certain transactions it will often be the balance between give and take that decides how much energy someone will invest in a particular project and also how much satisfaction can be gained from doing such a project. Both factors will obviously influence the success and power of any particular transaction that is negotiated.

Think for a moment about any particular job or project where you did some work for which you were paid. Then ask yourself the question: *"What would have happened if the fee I received had been twice as much as I had actually been given?"*. Would this new arrangement have strengthened or weakened the whole transaction that took place (for both parties)?

And what would have been the case if the amount you were paid was 150% of or perhaps two-thirds of what you actually were paid. It is often possible, with such a 'price barometer' to indicate quite precisely what would be necessary to get the most out of such a transaction.

Once, to my acute embarrassment, I received the unlikely sum of € 1,500.– for one and a half hours of my time. This happened in a situation where I had initially been willing to do the workshop, for which I was paid so much, for free!

Often when I'm giving a workshop about systemic work in organisations to an interest group, such as divorce lawyers, I only ask for a somewhat generous contribution to my travel costs. For me in such situations the balance between give and take works as follows: I will be learning something from the new group of people I'm meeting and they will learn something new from me. Then it becomes a more fruitful collegial exchange, rather than a one-sided workshop that requires a fee. In such cases I feel it is appropriate that I just charge my travel expenses. Then I'm free and the participants of the workshop are free. I don't just have to give, but can take to an equal extent. Also, for that matter, I do just as much preparation for such a workshop as is necessary and no more. If, when two colleagues meet, they exchange one Euro they both walk away with one Euro. If two colleagues exchange an idea they both walk away with two ideas. That is how it works in this type of workshop. Everyone gets enriched.

But, going back to the € 1,500.– I once received – it was, in the end, actually an entirely appropriate sum to be given. It seemed almost impossible to me that I would be able to give a one-hour workshop on the theme of the congress, 'Parting rituals at work', including a demonstration of a constellation. Because of this I had initially refused the invitation but allowed myself to be persuaded at some point and ended up with a stomach ache for two weeks before the event!

How could I possibly prepare myself for those first few, critical minutes of the workshop I needed to give? As it turned out that workshop was so condensed, with so much energy and attention and interaction squeezed into just one hour, that the fee exactly reflected what had been exchanged during the workshop. Amazing!

> **"** *It's not so much about how much money you earn with an assignment, but more what you end up doing with the money after you've finished the assignment* **"**
>
> *Bert Hellinger*

3.3 Debts and feelings of guilt

If there is balance after any particular transaction of give and take then both parties in that transaction are free. They are free to then make the next transaction with each other or with someone else. This could, per-haps, be an different way to look at free-lance work: after each transaction everyone returns to being free again.

But, whenever there is debt involved you will stay connected together. 'Debt' is being taken here to mean: the need to even things out so that bal-ance can be restored. Old debts can start to gnaw away at you. They can keep you imprisoned in the past. An old debt can become transformed into feelings of guilt: "*I feel guilty*". Often guilt feelings are 'secondary' feelings. Secondary feelings can tend to trap you in the internal image of something that happened in the past. Thus trapped, you lose contact with present reality. It is just these sort of guilt feelings that make it im-possible to take action, leaving us paralysed. Feeling helpless you end up a victim. Other people may be willing to help you out of your predicament but, at the same time, they will often feel they are being taken advantage of by you. Guilt feelings, and secondary feelings in general, carry very little force or energy.

They are meant to keep you in the victim-state and they will bind a per-son to inner images from the past. They support non-acting. The interesting experience for those who are around such a person who is bound up in secondary feelings and who are willing to help such a person, the is often that the moment they reach out to help, their help is doomed to fail. It's not possible to help people while they are stuck in secondary feelings.

The solution in such a situation, where secondary feelings are at play, is to simply face reality: one person ended up getting more and for the other person it cost more. Period. End of story. That's reality, and it comes with all its particular consequences. In fact you can only really start to take action again when reality is faced fairly and squarely. In this situation you will need to fully face and acknowledge your debt in relation to the other person, and this is sometimes painful. It is especially painful if the other person has had to pay a high price. Secondary feelings disappear whenever someone comes into contact, in any moment, with the underlying primary feelings. Guilt disappears when you can fully face and allow the debt you owe. Primary feelings are what are connected to real events in reality. Based in such a primary feeling you can look out at the world around you and direct your energy towards the future and possible solutions for whatever situation you find yourself in.

Exactly the same will hold true for the person on the other side of the balance. This is the person who ends up with the lesser deal in any transaction. If this feeling of being hard done by becomes fixed and transforms itself into secondary feelings, then you are heading towards a situation where you will be stuck with the event of this transaction for ever. You'll start complaining and will end up feeling a victim of what happened. This is the doorway into true poverty. It doesn't seem possible to get the balance of give and take going again.

The exchange with the other person dies and you end up alone. As such a person you will, after a time, find yourself feeling that you do not really belong anymore.

In such a situation it helps to return to the moment when the imbalance all started. From there you can come to terms with what happened, without, in any way, feeling reproachful or even wanting to change anything about it. The other person got more than I did. That's that! That's just how it turned out. Too bad. By being in touch with this reality the primary feelings become accessible once more. One such primary feeling is the pain of injustice. Eventually this pain itself will pass. Once the pain is gone you may find a renewed force coming into your life and you'll be better able to stay in touch with the stream of life. New interactions will then also be possible again despite the fact that differences may arise again through these interactions.

3.4 Using affection to take revenge

The balance between give and take also works when an injustice is done to someone. In a situation where injustice has been created the person who has been unjustly done by will now feel the right or need to do some injustice to the other, the original perpetrator in return – or at least to demand enough from the other person to set the exchange of give and take back in balance so that they can both, again, look each other in the eye.

When, however, the person against whom the initial injustice was done chooses to do an even greater injustice or injury back to the other person, then this initial perpetrator will feel justified in doing an even greater injustice back in retaliation. Here we have the perfect formula for escalation.

When, however, instead of hurting the other person back even more than the hurt that was originally received, the person answers with some injustice that is slightly less, but still clearly and firmly delivered, the balance can be restored. Only when this has been done can both parties face each other without old debts or claims interfering. This is what is meant by 'affectionate revenge' and it is, in fact, a model of de-escalation.

Hellinger himself tells a story of his time as head-master of a school in South Africa where he found himself in trouble at one point. What happened was that one day a fairly large group of pupils from the school, who had been given permission to go on an outing, did not fulfil their agreements about going on the outing and turned up back at school hours late. Hellinger felt it was important for him to do something to prevent his position and authority as the head-master being compromised. He requested that the class representative come up with a solution as to how the pupils could pay compensation for what had happened - so that trust and authority could be restored within the school. The pupils discussed it together for a long time. Their first proposal Hellinger refused to accept. They got back together and after much further discussion made a proposal that they would paint one of the school buildings that was in need of a coat of paint. This proposal had Hellinger's approval. The pupils renovated the school building in their spare time and peace was restored to the school.

3.5 Freedom, dependency and dignity

It is remarkable how precisely our 'organ' for maintaining the balance between give and take can work. Some people make sure they always give just a bit more than they are receiving. For example, a business might always ensure that its clients end up always owing them something. This has the effect of not really allowing these clients to be free and, as a result, the clients may find it difficult to behave in an adult way.

There is one exception to the give-and-take balance mechanism that we have been describing here. In families there are, in fact, two different relationships at work. Between the partners – mother and father – the mechanism for maintaining a balance between give and take works just as we have been describing it. However, a completely different relationship exists between parents and their children. Parents give more and children take more. Children cannot ever hope to redress this balance, and they do not have to. They receive much and are able to take this. Children create a 'surplus' on one side of the balance by being able to do this. Then, later, as adults, children can use their accumulated surplus to pass on something to their own children in turn. Adults can also give their energy or talents to some common project that is serving the common good, without expecting much in return. This principle may also apply sometimes within educational establishments and with teachers. The students in schools and colleges can never really completely pay back what they have been able to receive there. They will, thus, feel obliged to provide some good for others with this surplus they have received. One way to honour teachers or the educational establishments where you have studied is by passing on or publishing insights you have come up with through your own work. New ideas can grow in this way and enrich society as a whole.

As well as having a direct impact on our sense of freedom, the maintenance of the balance between give and take also has a lot to do with our sense of dignity. I find this most especially when I work in those countries where people do not have a lot of money to spend. How much, for example, should the Kolchos-managers from White Russia pay for a management training, part of which takes place in the Netherlands? This is the sort of situation where the 'price barometer' turns out to be very helpful. Our inclination, at first, was not to require them to pay anything at all.

But had we set it up that way the Russians would have lost their dignity. We would have ended up feeling like 'parents' and the managers would have been forced into being 'children', thus totally invalidating the whole training. There would have been no force in the exchange between us. Once this became clear it was a simple matter to decide on what would be the appropriate fees to charge. As far as the White Russians were concerned they were making a considerable investment in this management training and their trip to the Netherlands thus was allowed to become a real study-trip and not just a nice outing.

3.6 Personal interest and company interest

During the time a person works for any particular organisation there will be a continual stream of interactions happening – with customers, with colleagues, with the employer and with the managers. Some people have work that involves a high 'turnover' – not in terms of monetary value but in terms of the number of exchanges of give and take that are happening and that continue to grow. Much given and taken or a high turnover in the number of give and take exchanges will both confer a feeling of richness.

If someone works in a position within a company where he or she is not able to create such a turnover in exchanges you may find such a person seeking out other ways to increase his or her personal rate of turnover. Someone might offer to work for the employees' union or become a support person for colleagues. If these activities end up benefiting the company everyone benefits. On the other hand, that sort of situation cannot last for long if only that person's personal turnover of exchanges improves as a result of these extra activities.

We see, when working with constellations, that it will always be the company's goals that prevail over the individual's goals - they are always stronger than everything else. Attempting to increase your own turnover of exchanges at a cost to the company will never succeed because the soul of the organisation's system will not accept this dynamic. Sooner or later someone will have to leave the company to ensure that this unbalancing process is brought to an end.

3.7 'If you love someone set him free'

If someone in a company possesses more talents than that particular company can make use of, or may want to pay for, it results in there being a lower turnover of exchanges than is potentially possible. Although there is always the balance of give and take, a person working below his capacity will still only be able to do this for a limited period of time. If this sort of situation carries on for too long the person begins to devalue himself and that eventually starts to gnaw away at his sense of general well-being. It is very important that managers, employers and employees recognise this dynamic. Sometimes an organisation will set up a fake position for such a talented person, just to keep him within the organisation. But, by doing this, the organisation ends up devaluing itself and so this, also, is not the real solution.

It sometimes works for the organisation to say to such a talented employee: *"We've noticed that you have many more talents than we can possibly make use of in this organisation or could pay you for. As far as we are concerned you are free to leave whenever you choose. But while you are still working for us we will certainly appreciate what you can contribute very much"*. With this having been said the talented employee might choose to stay on a bit longer, and be useful to that organisation until it ends up being time to move on to something new.

We also learn from these cases, that acknowledging an imbalance in give and take needs to precede the actual actions taken to restore the balance.

3.8 New growth and profit

It is also possible to see the concepts of 'growth' and 'profit', that usually only refer to 'economic growth', in a completely different light. Growth can take place through exchanges between a company and its environment, in the systemic 'turnover' of exchanges or in the ever-increasing power of transactions that can allow employees and customers to grow in dignity. Such growth frees up customers and employees, rather than making them more dependent on each other. Such growth also leads to a company that has the same qualities as a person who would have lived a rich and full life, establishing a wide circle of friends and contacts who thereby gains a more and more respected position in society. In an article written about Israel's 'businessman of the year', who happened to live in the U.S.A., the people who worked for him directly were interviewed and asked what they thought could be the secret of this businessman's success. Their unanimous answer was: *"He is generous. Generous to all: his employees, his suppliers, his business partners and his customers"*. This, obviously, is clearly someone who is creating a tremendous turnover in his give and take exchanges. He is clearly, also, someone who wants to use his great wealth to fulfil his responsibilities to society and in this way is able to do something about the problems in Israel.

The New Economy. How would the stock exchanges look in such a new economy? When would the rates rise? What would the balance between give and take look like for the stock holders?

3.9 Grants

A colleague of mine happily announced that she had been given a grant from the Dutch Embassy to provide trainings in Suriname, a former Dutch colony. Having completed these trainings she confessed: *"I will never do it like that again! The grant did not work out well. The Suriname people felt offended and I feel less and less happy about it all."*

Whenever you have anything to do with grants make sure there are no hidden third-party interests at work. Very often, if there is a third party somehow involved, this party will begin to make demands and thereby weaken any transactions that the grant is intended to create, removing any freedom from such transactions. What if, in this example of the grant by the Dutch Government to Suriname, there had still been some feelings of guilt on the part of the Dutch Government towards Suriname. That sort of guilt would 'infect' the grant because of its covert attempt to pay off an old debt to Suriname. This had, unconsciously, been felt by all parties involved in this grant.

In France angry performance artists disturbed the Tour de France. The French Government has an arrangement that performance artists who have worked for only two months in a year can have benefit from this for the remainder of the year. Such a deal has allowed these artists to devote themselves completely to their profession and their passion. The result is that France boast to having developed a tremendous amount of theatre talent, evidenced by the many high-quality festivals that take place throughout France. What happens if the French performance artists begin to see this arrangement as their right, rather than as a gift? Does this strengthen or weaken such an arrangement? If you receive a grant as a gift it becomes a friendly reminder that you will need to do something in return for others.

How do these artistes maintain their creative freedom? What allows them the greatest creative impulse and how can the public and society in general receive and absorb this creativity? Do these rights, that have been achieved through conflict, actually give the artistes more dignity? Or do they eventually end up weakening the whole arrangement, turning the achievement of such rights into some sort of Pyrric victory?

With grants that become 'learned', or established as a right through some sort of conflict or argument, the recipients of such a grant will inevitably feel better than those who are giving the grant. It would be much the same as when a child would claim the right to receive from its parents. That sort of arrangement won't last long at all! Working with constellations I've noticed that in some cases the giving of a grant to an organisation strengthens that organisation and in other cases an organisation's work can become weakened by receiving a grant.

A good starting point for all of this is that the balance of give and take, whether or not subsidised by a third party, should not only bring pleasure to the work being done, but also bring pleasure and energy to the whole interaction involved.

3.10 Benefits

One constellation that many people have been moved by was one that involved a woman who lived on a disability pension. She wanted to do some research into the possibilities of returning to work and of receiving further training. She had formerly been head of a school and wanted to find out which direction she should go in professionally that would give her most power.

In the constellation we set up a representative for the disability pension scheme itself and this had a very beneficial influence on the whole constellation. The woman said she felt very much supported by the disability pension scheme and that it was important to acknowledged that here in the constellation. She had received a gift and done some good with it. It gave her exactly that freedom, support and energy she needed to re-shape her working life. But to the outside world she had felt herself to be a victim when she had ended up with a disability pension. Everyone participating in the constellation was moved by what they saw and in that moment were able to see the disability pension scheme and its possibilities in a completely different light. The question as to whether such a disability pension scheme actually gives power or takes away power from those involved in receiving a pension needs to be determined on a case by case basis. Here is another example.

3.11 Whiplash

A woman took a training to become a management consultant and then entered the navy. Shortly after that she was involved in an accident during a naval operation and could no longer continue to work as a consultant. As I had been one of her trainers in her training to become a management consultant she wrote to me asking me if I would be willing to make an assessment of her potential. She hoped, with this assessment, to support a claim for compensation that she was going to make against her employers before she left the navy. She was obviously very emotional about the whole thing.

I wrote back to her saying that, to the best of my knowledge, I would estimate her potential to be that of a manager of HR department in a mid-sized organisation.

I added two more sentences, with some hesitation, to my letter: *"What means more to you - a life with or without the whiplash?"*, and: *"If you were, at this point, to receive compensation from the navy would that eave you being more or less bound to your former employer; weaker or stronger as a result?"*

Some time later she sent me a thank-you letter together with a gift. She wrote to say she really appreciated my estimation of her potential, but that what had touched and helped her more were those two last sentences in my letter to her.

3.12 Second generation issues

A very energetic and competent female manager, working in the centre of Amsterdam, was in charge of a group of employees. She was wondering why these particular employees seemed to be producing results at a level less than might be expected, given their experience and training. It turned out that several of these employees were Jewish and were receiving benefits from a fund set up to provide for the relatives of victims of the Holocaust. At one moment this manager realised that perhaps the benefits these Jewish employees were receiving could be contributing to their feeling that they are also victims and thus it was limiting them in their performance at work. With this insight she was able to take a very different view of the strange problems she had been having with her team of employees.

Where is the boss?

4

> **❝** *Someone will become authoritarian when he uses more power than he is entitled to through his position or personal weight. By doing this he will forfeit his authority.* **❞**
>
> *Bert Hellinger*

Probably the most basic requirement for any organisation to be able to grow and flourish is that the role of leadership within that organisation is assumed in the correct way. On the whole leadership really comes down to order. And true order is order that simply works.

4.1 The first place

Hellinger: "*The most important person in any organisation is the owner. He or she will create the structure within which everyone else can function. This may also be a general manager or board of directors. This explains why management must respect the owner of an organisation or the board of directors.*

When an owner and the management have mutual respect for each other they will both feel free to do what seems appropriate in any given situation. In essence the manager is offering a service to others. In any organisation a very significant question to ask would be: 'Is the manager of this organisation using his or her authority to serve others?'. Authority can be accepted when people find they are being served by that authority. Authority will be rejected when the person in authority is exercising power over others without serving them."

4.2 Three principles of leadership

The first principle of leadership: the person who creates the framework within which others can function, must come first. After this position would come the person who creates the framework or structure for the following group and so on. A systemic hierarchy.

The second principle of leadership: that those groups of professionals who contribute most to the achievement of the goals of the organisation would come before the groups of professionals or functions that merely support these goals. As an example, in a district health centre the G.P.'s would come before the physiotherapists, who would come before the dieticians and other paramedics.

The third principle of leadership: seniority. The person who has been working the longest in an organisation has precedence (systemically) over someone who comes in later.

You will quite often see these principles as uneasy bed-fellows in hospitals. The person who creates the income that keeps the hospital running will come first. These, however, are not usually the medical specialists. The health insurance companies and the Department of Health are also important elements in the system of any hospital and health care in general. This will also always be the case for donors and those financing organisations.

Sometimes it is clear that one organisation has an important role to play in setting up the necessary structures for some other organisation to be able to function well. My wife once, in a workshop for teachers, set up a constellation that included not only the school but also the local education authority and the Department of Education. By doing this it became clear just how fundamentally important these other two organisations were for the school itself.

When donors and others who are financing non-profit organisations are thought about in a condescending way we can too easily lose sight of them or even unconsciously exclude them.

4.3 Putting things in order

It turned out that the woman actress who was taking care of the planning and organising of grants for new productions in a theatre company ended up being in the first position in the system. This had only happened gradually and she was obviously moved when her actual position within the system became clear during a constellation and was thus able to be acknowledged. She had not been the founder of the theatre company, but had joined the group later. Oddly enough their business manager was not part of the system of the theatre group. She was more in the position of a coach or consultant. Acknowledging this reality allowed the theatre group to start developing new projects. In that sense reality is always friendly. When we come to terms with this we come in touch with reality and this allows something new to appear. This is not always the case with dreams, illusions and our internal pictures, with complaints and accusations and other ideas about reality. These will paralyse us, keeping us from what is essential and therefore from being able to act.

I myself have discovered that legal structures do not always coincide with systemic structures. I worked in an organisation once where, having worked there for a certain length of time, you could be invited to become a partner in that organisation. Naturally I had had the ambition to become a partner and to be one of the decision makers in that organisation. On paper all the partnerships were equal and had the same rights.

The partners who joined the organisation later were also given equal opportunities to make their ambitions come true. For this reason the various portfolios were regularly reviewed. Nevertheless I had always felt during those years I was a partner, that I was actually in paid employment. Despite my ambitions and my involvement in the company I never really felt like I was an entrepreneur. The two partners who had taken over the company when the original two founders left had always been number one and number two in the company. Not because they were in any way behaving as 'kings of the castle' but simply because of the income they were able to generate for the company through their work. So when this started to get to me a little and I wanted to be my own boss I realised I would have to leave and, since being on my own, I feel only now am I a real entrepreneur.

I think, essentially, it has to do with the fact that any entrepreneur is required to make decisions that involve an element of risk. If you can survive that, it gives you a certain strength. The owner of a company will end up in the first position in a system simply because the decisions he or she is required to take – about the survival of the business, those working in the business and their families etc. It is obvious that the owner is taking these risks in the service of many others who might be involved with the company. Facing the possibility of making a profit is not so difficult to do. Facing possible loss, however, and being prepared to face possible loss, give a certain strength.

4.4 Leading from the first or from the last position

If a new managing director arrives from outside a particular organisation and is hired because of his competence he can lead the board of directors from either the first or the last position in the system.

 If he leads from the first position he will take first place and determine the structure within which his fellow managers will need to function. This is comparable to a parent who creates a certain structure for her children. The manager says: *"I am in front. I take the risks. I decide and I will explain my decisions and do this for the benefit of the whole organisation. I rely on you to do the same and to cooperate in this way."* If the new manager leads from the last position in the system he will address the other managers with the attitude of: *"You have been here first and longer than me. You have contributed much to this organisation. We will keep what is good and useful and change what is necessary to be changed".* He listens to what everyone else has to say and then decides.

> **"** *Don't change what works.* **"**
>
> *Gunthard Weber*

4.5 Self-managing teams

Perhaps you work for a team that is self-managing. This week I met such a team, at a French para-gliding school. (Note: Para gliding is just as reckless an activity as doing constellation work. It is flying with a large piece of cloth, using a huge number of different strings attached. The forces in the wind are much greater than the individual para glider pilot can hope to handle. You cannot see these forces but you feel the effects of them working on you very directly. If you fight against the dynamics of the air currents, you are lost. After years of experience, you start to get a feeling of what is going on when you are up in the air like that. If you can move with the forces that are there, without submitting to them completely, flying is a very special sensation, humbling and awesome at the same time.

But never forget for a moment that there are unseen, life-and-death forces also at play.)

I went to this para gliding school to check out if I could take an individualised course. I asked the first instructor I came across on the landing-field for the boss. *"Wrong!"* he replied. *"We are all equal and so you can discuss anything with me"*. Which I proceeded to do. Eventually I flew with the 'systemic' boss of the school. He was the one with the greatest overview and, without really being noticed, was coordinating the whole team. Although, in the experience of the flying instructors, this was a self-managing team, there was certainly a leader from the systemic point of view.

Up until now I've often seen that the leadership question becomes an issue sooner or later within any self-managing team. This will tend to happen sooner in teams where a lot of energy goes into considerations with each other and the making of decisions. What happens is this energy is then no longer available to do the necessary work. Self-managing teams work fine if a strong leadership exists somewhere outside the team itself. This should not be just management, but actual leadership. The sort of leadership that will watch over the whole team itself, that is there but not doing anything itself and, indeed, is creating the structure within which the team can function properly. In this situation the co-workers in such a team will be able to work out together how best to allocate the necessary tasks.

4.6 Where is the boss, actually?

Well, where is the boss, actually, speaking systemically? Even if he (or you, if you are in charge) is behind his desk and the door is wide open, he may be giving his attention to many different projects in any one given moment.

Once upon a time I was manager of a department in some back-water of a multi-national company.

I was asked to take on managing a second department until a new manager for this department could be found. I was told that this might take some time. Since managing this second department was not a full-time job I could easily include it with managing my other department.

A few months passed before the niggles and complaints began come in my direction from those in the second department. They were pointing out to me in subtle ways that I needed to cut through some things. According to them the people in this second department were feeling that I was not really involved much with them. Where was I then? In my heart I was more involved with the first department. But I was also only half there because, on top of everything else, I was part of a very interesting, nation-wide team project. In the end I did, indeed, leave this multi-national and in retrospect it is a miracle that the employees in both the teams I was managing were loyal to me for so long. If you pose to anyone in an organisation the rather strange question: *"On whom or on what does the boss have his or her attention?"* everyone immediately understands what you are talking about. Is the leader directed towards his employees? Is he directed towards his own boss? Does he focus on something outside the organisation, maybe a new job? People in organisations feel unerringly to where, systemically, the boss's attention is going.

A woman from a management team did not think much of her boss, the town clerk. But she had another problem too – another manager colleague. Or, to put it more precisely, the employees in her department were always getting into trouble with the employees from her colleague's department. He himself was a regular chap, but, despite many discussions little changed in the problems these two departments had with each other. The problem revolved around defining tasks. Work, belonging to one department, was being done by the other department, and vice versa. The situation demanded some sort of decision to be taken.

Whenever the subject was broached this woman would every time just draw a blank with her boss, the town clerk. She described the town clerk as being competent, efficient and even a ambitious woman. The manager we were working with had used all her available resources to support the town clerk in coming to a resolution for this problem, but nothing really had happened as a result. In a very simple constellation that we set up we saw that all the representatives, like a group of partisans, with the town clerk at the front, were all looking in more or less the same direction. The town clerk could not see her managers, let alone her employees and besides that, she was fascinated by and very actively attentive to something in front of her. The manager who set up the constellation was a little upset when she saw this picture. She held up her hand in front of her mouth and said: *"Yes, this is true. We are busy with a very ambitious project that is supported by all of us. But, in this way, there is not really anyone left who is keeping an eye on the organisation as a whole and who sees what is needed there".*

4.7 How high and how far away is the boss?

If you are the boss yourself you tend to think that you are human, closely connected to your employees and that, in some way, your door is always open. But how far are you in reality from your employees?

Perhaps this is a good topic for a work performance meeting? Take pieces of paper that will indicate representatives for the groups of employees and the boss. Write down on each piece of paper the function of the person that this piece of paper represents. Don't talk about the people themselves, but give them the names of their functions: head of department, team leader ICT, assistant ICT, book-keepers, etc. People are employed, in a function.

This means that a part of their personality and their potential is present and available to the organisation. If you would set them up as a person, they would be far too exposed. This is also not how it is in reality. From the systemic point of view the only thing that is important is the function that a person has in the system and how this function relates to other functions. If we forget this we will tend to move away from systemic work and enter the field of socio-grams and even further away from systemic work – ending up with the sensitivity trainings of the '70's.

Write out these functions on pieces of paper. Not all employees need their own piece of paper. Sometimes you can create groups of employees, with more or less the same function in the system, that will be represented by just one piece of paper. Mark on the paper an arrow that indicates the direction this particular representative is looking. Then ask an employee, based on his or her feelings, to put the pieces of paper on the table (if you are using A4 format, on the floor) in a way that represents the reality of the organisation. Look at the relative distances between the employees and the leader. This paper image will give a first impression of your position as a manager of the department. Perhaps other employees can also make an image of the system of the department using these pieces of paper. And it could also be useful for you, yourself, to sometimes do it too.

Find out what effect it has if pieces of paper are slid in a particular direction or to a particular position. How can the various employees function best? How can the department as a whole function well? It may just seem to be a bit of a game, so only do this when there is some serious intent present.

4.8 The rescuer: how to make sure you are not landed with this medal

Some years ago the manager of an engineering business made sure that when his business was taken over by a much larger engineering business, that this business, now a subsidiary of the larger company, could retain its original name and continue to operate fairly independently.

A few years after this merger, tensions started to arise amongst the managers. The department heads, who made up the management team, together with the managing director, felt as though they were relating to the managing director as little kids. They felt constantly controlled; the boss kept an eye on everything, and it resulted in the department heads feeling completely paralysed. On the other hand the managing director was complaining that the heads of the departments were not taking enough initiative and were coming up with very few workable proposals, despite having been regularly encouraged to do so by him. A deputy managing director was appointed but he, too, could not close the gap between the two parties. He may have been a manager but he was not a leader.

Part of the dynamic in this whole situation arose from the fact that the managing director at one point had saved the business from collapse. It had been a remarkable achievement. However what turned out was that, without in any way having intended it to be so, the managing director found himself set up on a lonely pedestal. He had not realised that this is what had happened and he certainly did not want it to be this way. It became almost impossible to bridge the gap between him and the heads of departments and again, against their will, the department heads ended up behaving like children.

You could say that the managing director here has been identified as the saviour of the business, and is thus placed on a pedestal. This is the sort of situation where a ritual can become part of the solution. The person of the managing director is hereby 'de-identified' with the function of saviour. It is still possible after this ritual to acknowledge the remarkable achievement the managing director had once made, but the battle is now over. The former hero can continue as managing director, with all his human failings and qualities and, together with the other heads of department, they can now turn their attention to the future.

4.9 Leadership and network organizations

Constellations sometimes don't work out. No clarity is achieved. The dynamic that becomes apparent in the constellation has no obvious explanation and there is no way out to a solution. Nevertheless, sometimes even these 'failed' constellation can provide special insights. This was the case in the following constellation.

A consultant asked if he could have a private consultation with me outside the workshop. He was having trouble with one of his colleagues and actually wanted to be rid of her. This colleague was also in the workshop so I, with mixed feelings, promised to work with him after the workshop finished. The consultant brought along his partner to this extra session, who is also a consultant. They had founded a business together. This consultant, who seemed to be more the number one, formulated the following question: *"Is it better for the business if this female colleague leaves?"*

When I asked them if they had already decided to dismiss her, they, hesitatingly, denied this. I should have stopped at that moment. I should have felt that really what they were wanting was for the decision to dismiss this female colleague to be made by something outside themselves – by perhaps me or the constellation. A constellation does not help if someone has already, internally, made a decision. A constellation cannot reduce the consequences. The decision maker has to bear the full consequences of any decision and in full view of those implicated by the decision. But, I was enticed into continuing, motivated by the idea that I was somehow connected with the system as a whole, not just to these directors. So, we carried on. In the discussion with both partners it ended up with partner one setting up representatives for himself, the second partner, the woman in question and the company.

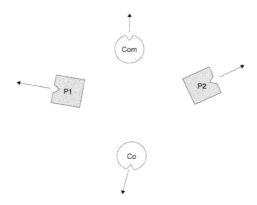

P1 = partner 1, consultant
Co = colleague, whom they might want to dismiss
P2 = partner 2, consultant
Com = company
A square represents a masculine principle, a circle repre-
sents a feminine principle

What we then saw was that each of the representatives began to sag at the knees. They felt miserable and felt like going outside. It looked just as though a bomb had exploded in the middle of the constellation or was about to explode. The company had been in existence for three years. There is no information about something that might have happened in the history of the company that could explain this constellation. So I stopped and puzzled.

Then it suddenly occurred to me to see what would happen if we were to replace the representatives with the actual people.

So I lined up both partners next to one another and behind them was the representative for the company and in front of them the female colleague, who was facing towards them. By doing it this way I was hoping to get some idea of what dynamic was at work here.

The representative for the company now felt okay. It was strange that the partners did not in any way seem to assume responsibility for telling the female colleague what was expected from her and what were the various relationships within the system. Both partners looked rather like adolescents and the female colleague felt like she could play with them. So I stopped again.

Just at that moment partner 2 said: *"We cannot dismiss her. We are a network. We can only ask her to leave".* This made it clear for all those involved. Partner 1 recounted that actually, with seven colleagues, they are seven separate companies. The 'company' was the network that these seven companies have created together. This sort of construction had the tendency to fly apart, as had been demonstrated by the image created in the first part of the constellation. Partner 1 and partner 2 were always focussed on the company, the network.

They continually are asking themselves what is best for the company. The constellation made it clear that the company had very little power and that both partners more or less hid behind the company. In doing this they lost all of their power and leadership for the company. The construction was neither one thing or the other. It was neither a company nor a number of strong consultants, each of whom were taking personal responsibility for the construction. It was, in fact, remarkable that both partners, as well as the colleagues, who as much as I knew them, were strong and competent individuals, were all weak in the network.

In the discussion afterwards the suggestion was made that two possibilities could be explored. The first was to have a different legal construction set up, whereby an actual company was formed. The second possibility was to stop with the network and for the consultants, with their own responsibilities, to work on each contract that came into the company as joint ventures with each other, having set out the clear conditions under which they were to work together. The latter scenario would end up with there being seven separate companies, each one being free.

Constellations that do not seem to bring much clarity to a situation sometimes carry hidden messages. In this case it suddenly became clear what the difference is, systemically, between a network and an organisation.

Networks are joint ventures of professionals. The network can share secretarial support or office space and clients are offered more continuity and security. More specialities are available and, if need be, people can step in and replace one another. But ultimately everyone is his or her own boss. The conditions for long-lasting success, placed on any network, are much stricter than those placed upon an organisation. Systemically-speaking most networks are not organisations but simply a number of people together.

If someone leaves, this changes the constellation. This is not the case with an organisation where, if someone leaves, the constellation, in principle, remains the same and all that happens is that the place of a function becomes free. What we have seen up until now, in our work with organisations and networks, is that, after 3 to 5 years, the leadership question starts coming up in networks. This could be the moment when a network is wanting to become an organisation.

> **"** *If the founder is not respected, this has an effect on morale of the labour force and on their identification with the company: both are reduced.* **"**
>
> *Bert Hellinger*

Living in a family business

5

If you work in a family business, does that qualify as working in an organization or is it more living in a family business? What are the secrets of family businesses? How can you find a good place for yourself in such a business? Where can you easily take part and what places are best to avoid? What are some of the ways in which you can get a good feeling for what is going on in a family business? Let's take a peek behind the curtains of family businesses.

A marketing manager was hired from outside a business. He took over the position that had previously been covered by the eldest brother in the family business. The eldest brother had been removed from the family business by this three younger brothers. This worked just fine for the new marketing manager for about a year. Then he went off for a few days to a conference in London. When he got back his office had been taken over by one of the brothers. The marketing manager was dismissed!

This had happened even though he was fully aware of the dangers involved in taking a position in a family system in which he did not really belong. Although the elder brother had been dismissed from the family business with a fight and the new marketing manager had been welcomed to his job with open arms, the family system still seemed to be stronger than just the business system itself.

Being loyal to the family dynamic, with all its malice, appeared to be the stronger mechanism at work than the alluring profits waiting to be made by the business with the hiring of the dynamic, enthusiastic marketing manager.

For anyone working in a family business the number one question is: *"What is running this business – the family dynamic or the organization dynamic?"*

Eighty percent of Dutch businesses are family businesses. One hundred thousand of these family businesses will be faced with the question of succession in the next ten years. Family businesses, in which the family dynamic is uppermost, have a number of different qualities to them than normal businesses. This also holds true for family businesses that have changed into being 'normal' businesses. Family businesses are more concerned with long-term survival. The fact that the business exists is more important than exactly how it continues to exist. There is, for instance, less emphasis on generating large profits than on continuity. Family businesses are more prepared to carry losses and tighten their belts than other businesses.

We know those businesses where you are more or less part of the family when you become an employee and where the whole family is at work: fathers, sons and daughters. They are concerned with 'life-long' employment. Such an employee will be likely to introduce him or herself as: *"I'm a ..."* followed by the name of the company for whom they work.

A board member of a family business once confessed to me how much trouble he was having in formulating the 'grounds for dismissal' document for a quality manager. *"He actually just does not fit"*, was his explanation. The family dynamic and all the 'done and not done' codes eventually determine whether or not someone fits. Someone can find a good position for himself and enjoy his work in a family business if he is willing to acknowledge and respect the fact that he will be working in an organisation where, when push comes to shove, the family dynamic will take precedence over the logic of the organisation. In a way you have to consent not only to the fate of the business, but also to the fate of the family.

A certain business produces liqueurs. Their marketing manager came to a workshop with the outline of a scientific research project that would be looking into the possibilities of constellations and their effects on a business.

She did a constellation around the question of what effect would the launching of a new liqueur have on their present target group of customers. Six months later she reported back on the effect that the constellation had had. Among other things she commented: *"As a marketing manager I have always been more focussed on the here and now and short-term future. I've only been working here for two years and I always want to move too quickly. My whole orientation was changed by doing the constellation. The company I work for has existed for 115 years. I'm now much more conscious of the 113 year history that has shaped this company before I ever got here. My boss, the present managing director, is the fourth generation of the family that has always provided the managing directors. Having done the constellation I no longer see him as my boss but more as the field in which I am working".*

The actual working structure of a family business does not always correspond very directly to whatever may be written down on paper about its hierarchy and structure. The grandfather still shuffles in once a week.

Sitting silently at the back of the board room, just a nod of his head can be enough for the business plans of his successors to be approved or rejected. Even when the grandfather is deceased he may be called upon in name and even consulted in thought by those who continue the company. If this strengthens the business it is a good thing. There may be a few members of the management team who do not belong to the family. They will feel only too well how the family dynamic, as well as the business dynamic, extends beyond the visible parts of the management system. Brothers and sisters, who are not even working in the business, often feel responsible for what is happening there. In this way they constitute part of the 'hidden management'. Often it is these family members, the unofficial members of the family business, who come up with questions in a workshop. In all sincerity they feel responsible for the business and share both what is going well for the business and also any concerns that that business may have.

Martin is just such a person. Martin: *"I'm a bit concerned about the family business my father founded. I'm no longer part of the business but many of my relatives still are. The business is not going well and I would like to know what is going on".*

Jan Jacob: *"Do you have the impression that your father would give you permission to have a look at this?"*

Martin: *"Yes".*

Jan Jacob: *"Where are you in the family?"*

Martin: *"I'm the second child. My eldest brother was managing director and died from a brain tumour at the age of thirty-three. My father's brother also died of a brain tumour at about the same age."*

Jan Jacob: *"OK, then first we should set up someone representing you and someone who represents your father".*

Martin sets up the two representatives.

F= father, founder of the family business
M= Martin, son, no longer working in the business

The father looks down at the floor for a long time, presumably towards someone who has died.

Jan Jacob to Martin: "*Set up your brother*". Martin sets him up.

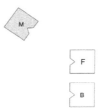

B= brother, who died at the age of 33, ex managing director.

The representative of Martin's brother feels himself to be larger than his father. Then Jan Jacob places the brother in front of the father, sitting down.

The representative for Martin is very watchful and alert. Jan Jacob now asks Martin to set up the business in the constellation. Martin indicates that the business is female, chooses a representative and sets her up next to the father, in the position where Martin's elder brother previously had been standing.

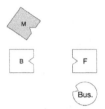

Bus. = the business that was founded by the father

Immediately it's clear from the way that the father and the business look at each other that, in the system, the business has replaced the father's wife. The representatives of both Martin and his brother feel a great deal of tension. Then Jan Jacob invites Martin to set up his mother, wife of his father.

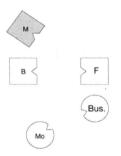

Mo= the client's mother and founder's wife

The representative for the business now feels larger than the mother. The mother feels pain. Then follows a ritual in which, amongst other things, the business says to the mother: *"I see you"* and *"I am sorry"*. Then the business bows to the mother. This feels good and at the same moment the mother and father sort of come alive. The difference is that at last the father is able to look around himself a bit. Martin, who is watching all of this taking place, is moved and says: *"Yes, that is how it was"*.

In this example we see how the mother has been excluded. For the father the business had come first and his wife came second. This has placed the children, who keep the business going, in a double bind: if they make the business successful they will be being disloyal to their mother. If the business collapses they will have been disloyal to their father. In some sense whatever they do won't be right. To make it right they will have to acknowledge and give a rightful place in the system to both the mother and the business. Seeing the representative of the business bowing before his mother had moved Martin and in this way provided a way for both parties to be integrated together: both mother and business can take up their rightful places within the system.

Jan Jacob let slip a remark: *"Perhaps it would be good to have some sort of monument for your mother placed somewhere in the business…"*. In the same way as we have seen here, relatives who have been excluded from the system can, in some way, end up being hidden governors. You cannot separate out the hierarchy of the organisation from the family hierarchy. If there are tensions in a business, often the family is lacking something. If the business system needs something very often permission is first required from the family system before this can be given. It is easy to see why these sorts of mechanisms sometimes make employees feel a bit helpless. Fighting the fact that the family dynamics are stronger than the organization dynamics does not help much either.

In such a business it will help if the employees can see the whole business in the context of the family, without necessarily wanting to understand or sort out all the complexities about excluded family members or family secrets. Such complexities and secrets are reserved solely for the family members themselves and they demand a certain level of privacy and intimacy. It helps those who are entering the family business from outside the family, to be able to see the business from the family's point of view. That is a kind of knowing without having any urge to have to change anything about what is happening. It also comes from knowing that you, too, have your own family in the background. Perhaps a family business has a warm heart for all families, for the families of all the employees and those connected to the business and not just the family of the family business itself.

5.1 Public property

Children who have grown up in a family business are sometimes faced with the difficult question – where are the boundaries between my family and the business?

My wife and I, after 25 years of working in our own separate businesses are now, for the past couple of years, working together all the time. Five years ago I would have discouraged anyone who was thinking of doing this. Now I find being able to work in this way a great gift. But it also has its consequences. Work can keep on going twenty-fours hours a day. To break out of this it is almost essential for me to physically leave and take a holiday somewhere. For my wife its enough just to get up and go out into the garden, which she thoroughly enjoys. If we are not very careful our house becomes our office and it is not always clear if a meal is a working meeting or a family affair. Our daughter (our son has just managed to narrowly escape and studies far away from home) told us one day that she no longer feels she can give the doors in the house a good old bang whenever our secretary is working there. This sort of thing really opened my eyes. What comes first, the family system or the system of work? Who serves whom?

A woman once told us that she had been born and raised in an institution, that her parents had founded, for the mentally disabled. For her, as a child, there had never been any distinction between the family and the institution. As a child she had been abused by some of the residents of the care institution and she said about this: "*I trusted everyone, like it was family*". Later at her work she was always needing to be aware of the separation between work and her private life. Even now she had the (unconscious) tendency to become intimate with colleagues and customers in contexts where such intimacy was not at all appropriate. One of the first steps we took in a constellation with her was to allow her to experience the boundaries between herself, her family and others. But we also have to be quite careful in such a situation to honour both systems, while at the same time separating them from each other without getting into new conflicts of loyalty.

We saw something similar to this situation with a man whose play-pen as a child was the space between four counters in his parent's shop. The children of parents who are shop-keepers grow up, in a way, as a kind of 'public property'. Later this can, either support or hinder such a person in their life at work.

It is a recognised fact that a son-in-law will ruin the business of his wife's family. I'm not sure if any actual research has been done into this phenomenon. Observations we have made in constellations indicate that, very often, the son-in-law, systemically speaking, does not belong in his wife's family. If he does happen to take over the family business it is a very good idea for his wife to take essential decisions regarding the business.

The woman stays number one in such a system and the husband is number two in the business. It remains to be seen as to whether the relationship between the woman and her husband can tolerate such a dynamic.

If a family business is handed over, for example, because there is no successor from within the family, it is a very good idea for the founder of the business to give his or her full blessing to whomever is taking over the business. I vividly recall the image of an modest, older gentleman who was at a workshop. He had founded a construction company which grew into a large and successful enterprise. He was at the point of wanting to stop with work and to take his wife on a round-the-world cruise. He had, in fact, already got everything organised but somehow seemed to still be avoiding something. He did a constellation to find out exactly what that might have been. The one thing he ended up wanting to do was to introduce his wife to the company. He stood proudly next to the representative of his wife and opposite the representatives of his successor and employees. He introduced his wife to them, thanked his employees for what they had done for the company. Then he turned to his successor and said: *"You can take over. I entrust you with the company. What I've set up you can lead further in your own way"*.

The man was beaming, the employees were beaming and the successor was so moved he could not say a word. And it was just the same for all the participants in the workshop who were witnesses to what had happened.

Organisational
change

6

Now that we understand so much more about the dynamics of organisations we are confronted by the question of whether we should be taking these systemic dynamics into account when thinking about organisational change.

The following case-study illustrates just how valuable it can be to check out what the dynamics are that might be dominant in any particular organisation.

An organisation consultant had a contract to supervise the change process that a municipality department was going through. This part of the organization was responsible for the contacts made with the citizens of the town. One of the three teams in this department would need to be transferred to another department. The two remaining teams would be working more directly with the public. The department head was ill and would not be returning. The head of the main department, meanwhile, took over the management of the department, but he was not good in this position. The consultant was already quite far into the project and one of the things that remained for her to do was to make a job-description for the new head of the department.

Firstly the consultant wanted to know what exactly was going on and whether there was something that would be important for her to take into account at this stage of the project. We set up the three existing teams, one representative for each team, plus a representative for the department head who was ill, one for the head of the main department and, later on, a director (the boss of the head of the main department) and an alderman (who was responsible, politically, for the work of that division). The teams were doing fine.

They were facing the public and their work and actually did not seem to care much about the management and managed their own affairs quite well. The third team was rebellious and arrogant. The consultant mentioned that this team was the one scheduled to be transferred to another department. The head of the main department stood out the most. He could not move, he saw everything that was going on but remained completely stuck. He also was not really available for his own teams or to the department head away on sick leave. It became clear that this feeling of stuck-ness had something to do with the director and alderman. But, since we were now touching on areas outside what the consultant had been asked to advise upon, we felt it was not appropriate and that we did not have permission to go further into what was going on at the level of the managers of the departments and the political board. After a small ritual of acknowledgement the over-burdened head of the main department felt much better. It was very valuable for the consultant to see what was going on and the constellation had provided her with not only recognition of the current situation but also with a great deal of new material and information that she could make use of. On the following day of the workshop the consultant really wanted to have a look at what the job-description might be for the new head of department. In order to do this we set up what is called a 'design' or 'scenario' constellation. We began with the last constellation from the previous day, that had been experienced by most of the representatives as being neutral. This means that most of the representatives felt more or less OK with their position in the system and no big hidden dynamics were interfering in the background. Then we set up the function of the department head. This was not the present head of department, nor the future head as a person, but the actual function of the head of department. We tried out three different positions for this function to find out what effect each position would have on the system as a whole.

Both teams were not happy with the function of department head in position 1. They could tolerate the head but would carry on going along their own track. The department head in this position was experienced as a sort of 'foreman'. They didn't need such a boss. Both teams felt this would threaten the considerable autonomy they presently enjoyed. They had, over time, developed their team to be pretty well self-managing. The others in the constellation also reported that they felt this was not a strong position for the head of the department.

Both teams experienced themselves as mis-trustful when the department head was set up in position 2. They were afraid that the head of department would also neglect them, just as the head of the main department had done. There was also, instantly, a tension set up between the head of department and this head of the main department, as though there was one too many persons present. Also position 2 was quite close to the burdened place where the head of the main department had been standing.

Position 2 was experienced as being one in which the manager was keeping an eye on the two teams, giving them assignments to do and checking up on the results. The representative of the alderman was continually making directive gestures with her hands, from where she was positioned in the constellation, when both positions 1 and 2 were tested out. She obviously was wanting something different.

In position 3 the head of department was fine for both teams. In this position the head of the department was shielding them a little from the alderman and the political influence on their tasks as civil servants. They felt supported, especially in what their principal tasks were as a team, by having a manager in this position. The alderman was also very happy with the head of department in position 3.

She felt that only now was she able to share her main ideas about the job of this division in working with the public more easily with the head of the department. The head of the main department felt fine too and said he would have no problem at all in working with the head of department in this way. He more or less functioned as a bridge between the political ideas of the alderman and the civil servant organization where his employees were fulfilling their tasks in this municipality.

Position 3 seemed to be by far the best position for the head of department.

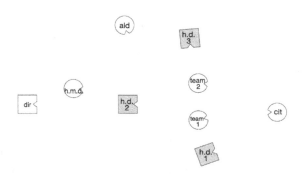

h.m.d. = head of main department
h.d.1 = head of department in position 1
h.d.2 = head of department in position 2
h.d. 3 = head of department in position 3
ald=alderman / dir = director / cit = citizens

What does all of this mean? We talked through what the consequences were of the three positions for the head of the department with the consultant.

Position 1 is the position of the head of department in the sense of being a manager. He manages both teams, is first in rank, keeps a tight rein on the teams and creates the structure within which they can work.

He also directs the way the team works and helps to improve and stream-line their work in this way. You can imagine what sort of job description would be needed for this position. You can get an impression of what sort of person would fit in in this position so you could specifically be on the look-out for such a person. It could, in fact, be someone who had already been doing the same sort of work that the workers in the team had been doing. It could be a strong 'primus inter pares' for both team leaders.

Position 2 is that of a someone managing from a distance. He would be more a supervisor for both teams. But the head of the main department is already doing very much that sort of function. In Position 2 the manager would be looking more at the results produced than at managing the actual way the teams were working. It would be quite a minimal function, certainly not a full-time job. It is a little bit like what the head of the main department is doing at the moment (but which he has no idea how to do). One of the functions seemed to be superfluous.

Position 3 is more like a liaison-function between the relevant requests from the city council, and the possibilities of both of the teams. This manager is also in touch with the target group, this being, in this case, the local citizens of the council. As well as being a liaison-function it is actually a service-oriented function that actually serves future developments of the council. The great advantage of such a function, that is directed more to the actual content of the work to be done and future developments, is that the head of the main department and the department, do not need to get in each other's way.

What was then interesting was that the consultant told us that her clients had actually wanted a job description that was more similar to position 2.

This was the function that a new head of department was being expected to carry out that the ill head of department and head of the main department had not been able to achieve, because of the dynamics inherent within the system. The organization was wanting to put in place a structure that the present dynamic will not allow to work. The consultant understood that if the organization appointed a head of department to fulfil the role that had been depicted as position 2 in the constellation that this would be an implicit vote of no confidence in the present head of the main department and the present head of department. It could mean curtains for the head of the main department and also any incoming new head of department could expect to have a very difficult time fulfilling his function adequately. On top of all of this there would be the chance that a new head of department lands up with exactly the same dynamics happening as his predecessor.

If we use this example to look at organisational change as a whole we can see that there are some far-reaching consequences. If there is a dynamic present in an organisation that is preventing it from achieving its goals, it is very important to first look at the dynamic and resolve this in some way before deciding to change anything. The systemic perspective is thus a very valuable one to look at in any process of change, together with the more standard organisational, financial and legal perspectives.

6.1 Three points to pay attention to in any organisational change

Whenever we are dealing with organisational change we need to have three main points on our checklist:

Firstly, is there a system dynamic at work that is so significant for any future change that we have to look at this first?

We have often seen in organisations that some presenting problem is not the actual problem, but in fact the experienced problem is the solution or coping strategy of the system that has arisen in response to some other hidden problem or system dynamic. Departments that do not co-operate well together sometimes are not able to, because of some un-resolved issue at another level of the organisation. If the chassis of a car is out of alignment, continually replacing the tyres ends up being a very expensive solution to the problem. The tyres are having to compensate for a bent chassis and that is why they wear out so quickly. The wear and tear on the tyres is not the actual problem but only an attempted solution to a problem somewhere else in the system. Performing a systemic check before any intended organisational change is a way of collecting important information about what is going on that can prevent simply trying to fight symptoms. This first point has to do with the question: is the system in this organisation actually ready to change systemically? Are there, in fact, not some dynamics present that might actually undo the benefits of any organisational change being proposed?

Secondly, does the intended change in an organisation have systemic effects on other parts of the organisation and how important are these side-effects?

Does the proposed change put people, departments or goals of the organisation into a different position within the system as a whole? Is the change going to remove from the picture something that, up to that point, had been very important for the organisation? It makes a lot of sense to find out what effects any proposed changes in one part of an organisation might have on other parts. With constellations regarding product brands we've regularly seen how the production and marketing of a new product by a company has great consequences for the relationships between important departments and managers of that company.

This is true even when, taking a superficial view of what is happening, these particular people should not be in any way directly affected by a new product being produced and marketed. Changing one part of a system has a ripple effect through to some completely different part of the system. This second aspect of change and system dynamics concerns the question: What is the effect of any change on other parts of a the system and does this change strengthen the system as a whole?

Thirdly, is the organisation decisive enough and able to change? Are the key people involved able to fully oversee, from their particular position within the system, the impact any changes will have? Are they in a position in which to be able to decide? Are these key people able to carry any consequences that may arise from any such decisions and do they have the power to implement the changes?

A well-designed organisational structure, designed by a consultancy firm, will have little or no effect on an organisation when the crucial people or decision-making units in that organisation are not able to take part in deciding what is happening and to guide any proposed changes to a satisfactory outcome. In this case the consultancy firm will be taking over the role of the director of the organisation and this leads to very different results that planned.

6.2 Changing while staying in touch with reality

For a short time I acted as a coach for the managing director of a waste-removal company. Well, coaching.... It was more like having conversations about the realities of life and work. He told me he had started out as head of a department in the local municipality that had partly been responsible for waste collection. This department had been privatised in those days when such things were the fashion.

This process of privatisation had been handled successfully by this ambitious manager who then put his mind to other possibilities in the market of waste removal. Very soon this former local council department had developed into a modern and innovative waste-removal company. The day came, however, when the dustbin men were no longer needed. The manager provided them with other places to work. He looked after them and thanked them for what they had done. He told them that, even though without them it would not have been possible to make the company into what it is now, there is no longer any room for them in the present company. At the farewell party for these men one of them said: *"You would have been an arse-hole if you had kept us on"*. That would have devalued them. This is an example of a change that stays in touch with reality. It is painful when a person is no longer needed. But it is also the truth. If this truth is not faced squarely, those involved start to live in illusion and with delusions. That weakens, everyone.

A systemic rule of thumb in any organisational change is that the system should only consist of those functions that are essential to achieve the goal and mission of the organisation. If you hold onto a function that is actually redundant you have a perfect recipe for excluding someone from the system, however strange that might seem at first sight. How often has it happened, for instance, in a merger of four small district municipalities into one large municipality, that four departments were created where the four town clerks could be heads of department, when in fact there was room for only three departments. Everyone knows that the fourth department is fake. Sooner or later this fact rears its ugly head and then the cost of this sham is actually higher than if clarity had been created from the very beginning. The costs of early retirement, re-training bonuses etc., plus the cost of lack of energy in the departments involved must all be accounted for later.

In that sense organisational change is a surgical intervention: *"I don't do what I can or want to do but I do what is necessary"*. Organisational change calls for courage, being a warrior and being ready to forfeit your innocence. At the same time is has something humble about it, being a service to the organisation as a whole and its role in society.

> **"** *An important principle is that an organisation is structured in such a way that nobody prevents anyone else in the organisation from doing his or her work* **"**
>
> *Bert Hellinger*

6.3 How do we rid ourselves of that out-dated goal?

The more you want to get rid of something the more you end up being bound to it.

Organisations have mission statements, goals, ideals, a particular house-style. These are important for the system of that organisation. They give it a direction in which to go, and ensure that everyone is working together. If times change, goals can change too and, as such, the goal or mission of an organisation is an important factor to take into account during any organisational development. We've repeatedly seen that problems often arise when the objectives of an organisation somehow get stuck.

Here is an example: The director of a social care centre, a woman, had experienced constant conflicts between her teams and the board of directors ever since she had taken on the job a few years ago. The fields of conflict and tension became immediately apparent when we set up a constellation.

It also became clear that something was missing and that this missing piece was actually the cause of these exaggerated tensions in the organisation. The question arose as to whether the religious roots of this organisation were important. The director then told us that the organisation had been founded by a order of nuns and was later secularised.

When representatives of both the nuns and lay people were set up in the constellation it had a big influence on all the representatives. The lay people refused to honour the nuns, saying: *"What is there here to respect?"* It became clear to everyone that the source of the tension in the present organisation came from here. In a way that was a relief. It was left up to the director to find out if and in what way it might be appropriate to give the founders a place in the organisation and to honour them in some way. Later on she told us that she had paid a visit to the nuns and had told them how the organization, founded by their sisters a long time ago, was now doing and how it had been developed over time. The nuns were happy to hear and agreed. Afterwards the director just casually mentioned her visit to her management team and somehow that seemed to have brought some sense of rest in the whole situation.

You will often find such problems in non-profit organisations that have been set up in response to some social need and from the ideals of the founders. If, after a number of years, the original objective of the organisation changes and this original objective is not somehow included in the organisation's gallery of honour, next to the portrait of the founder, then it will work in the same way as an excluded element of a system will work. Someone later may be hired to represent this neglected objective. Sometimes you can observe that the tension between two different objectives or ideals within an organisation, neither of which are respected, can show up as employees dividing into two opposing camps. They can unconsciously have become identified with both ideals.

What the actual content of the tensions between the two parties is can be completely different. The only thing that is being transferred, to people who have little or nothing to do with the origin of it, is the structure or pattern of the conflict.

Usually the founders of an organisation do not mind in the slightest that the objectives of their organisation change, at some later date, in response to the needs of the time. In constellations you find that representatives of the founders of an organisation even find it more uncomfortable if employees hold on too long to the original objectives. In these sorts of situations the organisation is stuck in the past and the founders cannot feel at peace. What is important to any founder of an organisation is being mistreated or excluded from the system. One of the best ways to exclude a founder is to place him or her on a pedestal and to worship him or her. That is a way to be bound to and haunted by the founder's original ideals.

6.4 Strong ideals isolate

Ideals that arise out of any form of criticism of society, need some special attention. As example, at some point in the past there seemed to be repeated initiatives to set up new sorts of schools. I happened to be teaching during that time at various schools that had been founded on strong ideals or particular opinions about society. In retrospect I have mixed feelings about all of what I did then. The primary objective of the school where I was a teacher for six years was to teach the pupils how to come into contact with society more. Working with projects and having all age groups working cooperatively together were the sorts of things felt strongly about. It was a great school but, as a teacher, it was extremely difficult – trying to maintain all those ideals the whole day long...

I also realise now that there was something else going on at the same time: we actually felt better than the other high schools in our town. We even felt better than most of the primary schools – as though we felt we had to re-do some of the kids' education again, which had been missed out by the feeder primary schools. Recently a parent had confided in me that in our city this 'ever-so-normal' school had been seen as an elite school: as if this school was felt to be the only 'real' school in the middle of society. Interestingly enough the ideal of the school was to be humble and for the school to be a mirror of society, of ordinary people. But the fact that they cultivated this goal as being so special in the Netherlands turned them into being an elite school that was focussed more on their ideals than on really meeting the children, their parents and society.

Whenever strongly held ideals require believing that other ideals are of less value you can be sure that part of the world is being excluded in some way. In the end you run the risk of becoming isolated. It makes a difference if someone starts up something new out of a feeling of being superior to others or because he sees a need and wants to serve to meet that need.

6.5 Orgenogram

Yes, you are reading it correctly! Orgenogram. We all know about the org. charts that show the structure of an organisation with indications of the leadership, the board of directors, the management and all the departments so that you can get a quick overview of the logical picture of what is going on. The org. chart gives you a picture of how it is at this moment in the organisation.

Sometimes dotted lines may indicate that perhaps one department is going to merge with another or if, presently, there is an unclear relationship between two departments. If we draw a genealogical tree or genogram of a family it will show the history of how the family came to be. This 'history of origin' is exactly what is so interesting from a systemic point of view because so many of the dynamics that are at play within any organisation at any moment all originate from something that happened in the past. Hence our introduction of the term: orgenogram. An orgenogram gives a picture of the history of an organisation.

A female employee of a large company went on a search. She called up the founder, who still headed up the company, to ask if he had an hour to spare to tell her about the original purpose of the company and how everything got started for this company. To her surprise he thought it was a marvellous idea. The employee felt there was something particularly intimate about hearing all these details about the beginnings of the organization and it changed her view and understanding of what was going on in the company. She quietened down a lot.

How do you put together such an orgenogram? Take, for example, the sort of small notepad which contains transparent paper that architects use. Start on the back page of the notepad, where you sketch the first org. chart of the organisation. This will include the founder, his ideal or objectives, the clients at the time the organisation was founded, the financiers or source of money for the organisation and other important parties who were involved. For each fundamental change that has happened in this organisation you take a new sheet of transparent paper and sketch the new situation as it was in that moment. It's perhaps good to put a date on each new page you sketch. The last, top page of the opened pad contains a sketch of the organisation as it is at the moment.

Below this sketch you will see the other, past constellations more and more vaguely filtering up through.

In the past we used to draw those little sequences of drawings that changed, little by little from one page corner to the next so that you would end up with your own little cartoon film as you let the pages whiz past your thumb: *"frrrrrt"*.

Such an orgenogram gives us a picture of the people and events that have made some special contribution to the organisation, of changes of direction or particularly significant happenings that had far-reaching consequences. You will also get a picture of all those people and families who have somehow benefited from the existence of this organisation or, on the other hand, have been damaged in some way or have lost their health. The social importance of this organisation will also come to light with such an orgenogram.

Our son visits old factory buildings as an 'urban explorer' and talks about this in an interview: *"I like old castles and I also like modern castles. If you walk around in these buildings you can sometimes even find old work rosters and you feel just how much has been lived and achieved in such a place".*

Some of the happenings or persons that show up in the movie or the orgenogram may still be essential to an organisation and its future. It pays to sketch out an orgenogram at the beginning of any projected trajectory of change in an organisation. What is important is to show the roles of the original founder of the organisation and any subsequent owners. These persons will be sowing the seeds, as it were, of all patterns for the future. The particular idiosyncrasies of the company will start here. The more authentic these are the more powerful they will be.

6.6 Systemic performance interviews

'Small' changes in an organisation are also worth our paying attention to. Shortly we will be needing to have our annual performance interview with our secretary. In the past this would have meant talking about how well everything is going and perhaps here and there a few things could be improved.

This would usually mean that I intend to make sure I'm clearer in my communications with her, and she also intends to improve a few aspects of her functioning. Since it is also an assessment interview (yes, I know, that assessment and performance interviews should actually be two separate interviews) I propose a raise in her salary and we make new agreements about the hours she will be working for us.

This year the need to look at this interview from a systemic point of view grew much stronger in me. Our business consists of the three of us. Systemically speaking my wife is, without a doubt, the manager, I am the owner of our business and our secretary has a supporting role. I've had the idea in the back of my mind for some time now. Would it perhaps be possible for the secretary to have a different position within the system, namely that of something like a organisational manager? So she would be more planning and actually creating the structure within which my wife and I could do our functions instead of just carrying out her tasks? Not having a completely clear picture for myself of how it might work I set up a constellation and was very much inspired by what was revealed: according to the constellation the arrangement of having our secretary function more as the organisational manager could have a very powerful effect on all three of us. Moreover, there would be the chance that our secretary's obvious potential for being able to look ahead when organising things.

This was a possibility which we were only minimally making use of at the moment, could be much more fully exploited.

So you can imagine that systemic performance interviews in organisations could also be done in this way. That factors that would need to play a role in such an interview would be:

- What position are you occupying at the moment in the organisation?

- Would another position (not function!) strengthen the department or organisation even further? Would such a suggestion allow the person's own productivity to increase? That would mean that greater use would be made of his talents, leading, in turn, to more interaction with colleagues and customers.

- On whom or on what could you, in your heart and mind, be more focussed?

- What balance of give and take would be associated with this other position in the department?

In this way you could imagine doing a whole systemic fine-tuning of a department. The manager would have a good systemic picture of the qualities (see also Chapter 8) of their employees and would thus be able to assign each one their appropriate tasks and activities.

Blood is thicker than water

7

What you bring to your work from your own family background

"Don't mix up work and private life". This advice often works well, at least at the level of one's daily activities. After work you switch off and have time to relax with your family and friends. In summary, when you are at work the job is number one and when you are at home your private life is number one. We are not talking here about all the workaholics and all those who handle family affairs during their working hours.

But, separating out work and private life is not actually quite that simple. Family backgrounds have a way of surreptitiously insinuating themselves into our working lives, whether we like it or not.

It happens much less frequently that the dynamics we are involved in at work get carried over into our family systems. This is mostly because the family is the primary system that forms us and work only comes later in our lives. Our family background, especially the dynamics of the family system, has a way of penetrating into our work situation a lot more often than you would expect, and most of the time, without us even realising that it has done so. Our family system can contribute, to a considerable extent, to who we are, what we are good at and in which position in an organisation we feel at home. But these family dynamics, that we are so wrapped up in our whole lives, can also end up holding us back in what we do at work. The family system is the number one pattern generator in our lives.

We are not talking here about the family norms and values that will colour our judgements in work situations and affect our attitudes to work. Some of these values, however, do have a profound influence on how we work: *"It is important to always work hard"*; *"Know your station in life"*; *"We can get through this together"*; *"You cannot afford to fail"*; etc. etc. These attitudes are fairly easy to recognise and often are a direct result of family circumstances. They come from the environment in which you grew up and you've taken them in with your mother's milk. Most of the time we are quite aware of these values that we have.

But what we are talking about here are the hidden dynamics in a family system, about positions we take completely unconsciously within the

---

system of a family and which, sometimes, all of a sudden, will work their way through into our working lives. That is what makes these dynamics so tedious.

7.1 The deceased twin-brother

A young, energetic and intelligent woman, working for a local municipal council, came to me for a coaching conversation. Despite being so young she was already fairly high up in the municipalhierarchy. She told me how each time she was just about to be successful she got into situations that ended up preventing her from enjoying those successes. It was obvious, in talking to her, that it was not her qualities and ambitions that were to blame. I asked her gently if I could perhaps find out some things about her family situation. She mentioned a number of significant events that had taken place in her family of origin but you could sense that these were not having much of an impact on her present situation. Then, suddenly, she said, whilst blushing, because she had only just now remembered something: *"Well, actually, a few months ago my mother told me I am actually a half-twin. My brother died at birth"*.

Tears immediately came to her eyes and you could feel that she was touched by something really fundamental here. A little while later, after a few more words were spoken, some of the puzzle pieces began to fall into place for her. She said: *"I always used to build rafts, climb trees, break my arms"*. If you looked closer at her you could see that Renée was not just a beautiful woman but also had something of a masculine quality shining through her. She said: *"There is something strange that I'm just realising now. My whole life I've thought that what I've always done is the same as what we call 'talking to oneself'. But, I always speak softly to someone else. Could that perhaps be my brother?"*

We then carried out a small ritual. I asked her to imagine her twin brother, just as though he was sitting right in front of her, and he is the same age as she is now. That greatly moved her. I asked her to imagine looking him in the eyes until she really could see him and until she could see that he saw her. Then I asked her to say, not out loud, something to him such as: *"Beloved brother, I missed you. I perhaps also partly tried to live your life. That might have given me a lot but it was also really hard.*

Perhaps I thought I won't do better than you would have done…". This last part moved her very much. I asked her: *"How would your brother look at you and feel about you if you were to do OK?"* She said nothing, but her face began to shine anyway, just like a small child's.

I suggested she do another simple exercise. *"Take your brother's hand, as it were, and show him all the beautiful things in life. And when you've done this enough, give him a place in your heart. That is a good place for a dear brother".*

Two days later I happened to be calling her about something else, because I was acting as a consultant with the municipality where she worked. She said: *"Don't ask me how I'm doing or what has happened to me. I walk around all day with a big smile on my face.*

I don't understand at all, but let's leave it at that".

I still remember this example because she later told me: *"I've been searching my whole life to find what it was that was causing me never to be able to succeed. I ended up at work in situations that I didn't ask for. I began to feel more and more guilty. It is such a tremendous relief just to know that it is possible for the cause of all of this to be something outside me and not in me myself".*

The 'family movie' is very probably playing itself out at work especially if you find situations where someone is continually being bothered by recurring patterns in their working lives. Situations such as: pitfalls you keep falling into, or excessively taking on other people's problems, without having any idea why these sorts of things always seem to keep happening to you, in particular. If you don't manage to recognise such patterns you will go looking in all the wrong places for a solution. The solutions won't be found in the work-place but in the family dynamics. But, also don't forget just how much family dynamics there are that can actually be a great support to us at our work. These also will happen completely unconsciously and we need to give our attention to this aspect of family dynamics too. Sometimes the very fact that we have had to endure painful and difficult situations in our family's dynamic gives us a certain set of qualities that qualify us to be able to take on particular functions or occupations at work. Someone, for example, who ended up in a position between the two parents in his or her family, may sometimes turn out to be an excellent mediator. Having a position in between the parents is not always difficult in your personal life and may cause some difficulties in the relationship with a husband or wife. But when someone has grown up in this position, he or she is almost bound to have developed many coping mechanisms to deal with such a situation. And these coping strategies can be of great help in our professional lives.

This is a way that a curse from one system can become a blessing in another system.

7.2 Father's daughters, mother's daughters, father's sons and mother's sons

The position you have in a family system sometimes requires you to develop a whole set of skills do deal with that situation. Very often these same qualities can turn out to be useful at work.

Mother's sons are, from within, more connected to the mother and all that comes from the mother's side. With some practice you can recognise such a person immediately. It is fun to practice this while sitting out on the terrace or among colleagues, with the proviso that you always check back to see if your observations are correct.

Mother's sons have the important assignment in their lives to save women, starting, of course, with their own mothers. They can easily become somewhat self-effacing. They get on with women relatively easily and they sometimes feel a bit uncomfortable around men who occupy a higher position than they do. This will certainly be the case for a mother's son who has been forced to some degree into the role of being his mother's husband and who has more or less completely taken over the father's place in the family system. A mother's son will do this, of course, out of a deep love for the whole system, but also, somewhere deep down, he will have the feeling that it is not right. *"If father is not available, I'll take care of you."*

It is sometimes amazing to see how a man will change when, at the end of a constellation, as a 'mother's son' he has, standing behind him, a whole line of men, and is feeling himself being washed over by the male energy and carried by this male lineage. This is how the son can end up projecting quite another, more masculine and powerful presence into the world.

Sometimes it is good, in certain work situations, to know all about this. Particular situations at work demand more of the feminine qualities of energy and other situations more the masculine type of energy. You can test this out in a constellation.

Father's daughters, are, by nature, more connected to their father or whatever comes through the father's side. Sometimes it seems as if they remain younger than their years, with a powerful aura coming through their femininity. They are often good as managers, but have the tendency to use this ability while in the employ of someone else, even though this is not always obvious on the surface. Sometimes father's daughters will attempt, in their work, to accomplish something that their father, or someone from their father's line, was not able to achieve. Women with older brothers find it easy to handle issues of authority at work. They know how to influence someone, who may be seen by others to be in authority, in a playful way. A daughter or son may end up between both parents in the family system, through having a sense that there is something missing from the relationship between the parents and therefore (totally unconsciously!) wanting to put that to rights. Such sons or daughters can become excellent mediators. They seem to find themselves getting involved, again and again, in situations where some form of mediation is called for. This is their way of staying loyal to the family system at work and it is an example of just how easily contexts of work and family can become confused.

Suddenly, while at work and without really realising it, you find yourself acting in your own family's movie.

If you want to get to the bottom of all of this the first step is to become aware of your pattern. But it is not really enough just to try to keep work and family apart. If, for example, you resist the temptation to constantly be stepping in, as a mediator, to sort out conflicts and problems between two other parties that are none of your business, you will end up with another sort of internal conflict: you are now becoming unfaithful to your own family system. It might help a little to be aware of the fact that you continue jumping from one movie to the other and back again, but a more complete resolution of the whole problem will only come when you take a look at what is going on in the family dynamic. Who or what was missing there, that resulted in a child being willing to step in between the parents? Family constellations can be a help here. The closer you can get to the source of a dynamic the longer-lasting will be any change that results from that understanding.

7.3 The hidden boss

A woman works in a large, commercial organisation. She has been asked by the management to initiate a change process, in which two teams would start cooperating together better. As part of this process of change she will end up being the manager of one of these teams, but it is not clear if she will also have some management responsibilities for the other team too. She is due to start work on this the following day and wants to know what is going on and what is her position relative to both of the teams.

In the constellation, having set up representatives for teams 1 and 2, a representative for the woman and one for her boss, it became very clear that it was a matter of leadership. The leadership is not been fully taken on and it seems that there is not really any place being created for the manager, who is the woman.

When this woman herself eventually took her place in the constellation she said to the other representatives, in a strong, forceful voice: *"I will do this job!"* The force and the resolution she showed in wanting to take on this job, against all the odds, amazed everyone present. The woman told us that in her family she had been the 'parent' of her own parents. When a child assumes the position of being the parent of her own parents in a family system she will behave as the person who is, unofficially, responsible. But she also has to hide this fact. This dynamic, that occurs very frequently in family systems, can often go on repeating itself generation after generation. Families can remain extremely loyal to this particular pattern. Children from such situations can start to feel responsible from a very young age and, despite the difficulties involved in such situations, they can gain a lot of strength from having lived in this particular pattern.

People with such backgrounds may sometimes take jobs in organisations while working on a hidden agenda – such as being the 'under-cover boss'. That is certainly a double-bind: unofficially being the boss and officially not allowed to take any decisions. It is not your place to make decisions and yet if you don't you are also in trouble. But in the case of this woman, the family dynamic from her family of origin provided her with the necessary force to fulfil her function within her organisation well. A curse, in this way, had become a blessing.

7.4 Carrying a burden for someone else

Perhaps you are someone who takes on tasks that do not belong to you or you take on responsibilities that only end up being a burden. You have been appointed to a job and you simply do not have the competence to adequately handle things. This is a bit unfortunate, but not such a big deal. It happens over and over again, in all sorts of situations. A hole appears in the organisation, a manager leaves something unfinished, a customer needs something urgently and there you go again, you are the one who ends up handling it. Eyes wide open, again and again, you act out this pattern, without a second thought. You only wake up to what you are doing when the burden starts getting too much to carry. There is a sort of love-hate relationship with such situations and it is the perfect recipe for a burn-out. Very often the roots of such patterns can be traced back to the family system.

It can happen that one member of a family carries a burden for someone else in the family. What is so painful about such a dynamic is that it happens out of love. A child feels that someone else in the family is suffering under some weight and says to herself: *"I'll carry it, so that it becomes lighter for you"*. Later on, as the child grows older she will start to blame the person for whom the burden was carried, or for whom some assignment was taken on. But it does not help to give back the burden in the mood of blaming that person. Doing it in that way does not change the dynamic, because you remain feeling bigger then the person to whom the load belongs. When a mother's nature is, in her soul, to be connected to her mother, who died young, then this woman will not be available for her own husband and her own children. In such a situation the oldest daughter of this mother will take on caring for the family, maybe even including caring for her own mother. This is a huge undertaking for a child to take on, but she will do it out of love, even when she has to pay a high price for what she is doing. The child is also not able to fix the family system, however badly she might want to do this. When she fails, as she must, she will end up with a double burden. It will only work out if, for example, during a family constellation, the grandmother of the family lets her own daughter (the mother of the present family) know that it does not help the grandmother in any way for her daughter to try and follow her to the grave. If this can be communicated to the mother then the mother can turn to look towards her own daughter. The mother can then see her daughter for who she really is and also be free to be a real mother for her. It is only in such a situation that the daughter, who has taken on the load from her mother, can return this load back to the mother. This feels very awkward for the daughter to do. Is it true? Is it OK to stop having to carry this burden? The daughter can be supported in handing back the burden to her mother when she can see that the mother will actually be strengthened by having to bear her own burden. Anyone who has been burdened by fate, such as a loss or suffering some personal guilt, actually grows in stature when she is able to carry such a burden herself. She becomes more dignified.

If you do have this tendency to carry a burden for someone or something else there is another factor that may well contribute to your ending up with a burn-out. It is that you actually never quite know when enough is enough. Because the burden you are carrying does not belong to you it is impossible to know when you are finished. You do not have any reference point with which to be able to judge such an end-point. So you just go on and on and on until you body finally decides to intervene. The pattern of 'doing someone else's job' is one of the best recipes for burnout. It certainly would be helpful for managers to be able to recognize such patterns in their employees at an early stage.

7.5 Double image

Sometimes the shift from work-movie to family-movie will involve only one person. We call this the 'double-image'. You have, for example, a tension or conflict with someone at your work or you feel stared at or judged by someone, for no apparent reason. To make it worse your colleagues do not share your feelings about this particular person. This can paralyse you and when anywhere near this person you feel you are less effective than you normally would be. And it's not even that you are in love, or anything like that.

What can be happening is that, unconsciously, something from the family situation has suddenly jumped across into your work situation. The person giving you trouble at your work is, as it were, a stimulus that sets your family movie rolling. But what is playing in the family movie may have nothing whatsoever to do with what is happening at your work. The family history slides, like a transparency, between you and your work. From that moment you are being run by your family situation and no longer by what is happening at work.

It could be something such as someone looks at his boss but, instead of seeing his boss standing there, he is actually seeing his father in front of him. He will not be aware that this is what is happening. Suddenly, he might feel all sort of clumsy, or it might perhaps even go as far as feeling weak or paralysed. Feeling so impotent he will tend to get angry with himself and blame himself for what is happening. The more he tries to find out what is going on between him and his boss the harder it becomes for him to see what is actually going on in the background. It is possible to recognise when such double-images are at play. In this example we are using, the employee would be standing opposite his boss. If you were to look closely at this employee in that moment, you would be able to see that, quite suddenly he looks very different when he is standing in this position, facing his boss. He no longer looks like an employee facing a boss, two adults opposite each other, but he looks more like a child standing in front of his parent. His look changes, his face becomes more like that of a child and, sometimes even, his voice will change too. Someone observing all of this, who knows the colleague quite well, might suddenly think: *"Hey, he seems completely different from how he was just a moment ago"*.

In a constellation used, for instance, in a coaching session, a double image is easy to see and resolve. To be able to do this you don't even need to delve into the family situation that is causing the whole thing. The facilitator will simply set up someone to represent the client and someone to represent the boss. He will ask the client to look at the boss.

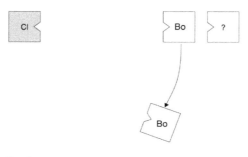

Cl = client
? = unknown person, possibly family member of the
client.
Bo = Boss

Someone of the same gender is set up behind the boss. After a couple of seconds the facilitator moves the boss, unobtrusively, but decisively, about a metre and a half to one side. That leaves the client now looking straight at the person who had been standing behind the boss.

The facilitator is watching the client's face and posture for any changes and then asks: "*Who is this?*" If this process sets off some strong or emotional response in the client (who may answer with something like: "*My grandfather*") then we know we are dealing with a case of a double image. If this is the case the facilitator would have the client look alternately between the grandfather and the boss. The representatives are standing just far enough apart that the client is not able to see both of them at the same time. The grandfather would then say: "*I am your grandfather and he is your boss. We are two very different people and we have nothing whatsoever to do with one another*". The boss could then also say much the same about the grandfather. Finally the facilitator would ask the client to say to the boss: "*I've been confusing you with my grandfather. I'm now beginning to see you as my boss*". The way this is said, of course, would be adapted to what feels right for the client.

7.6 The hidden spectator

A trainer was once confessing during a workshop that in certain training situations with a group he would sort of lose himself. This would happen most especially when he had the feeling of "*I should know what to do here*". At the moment when he was telling us this we were actually working in a group with him so it was not difficult for him to imagine himself back in a situation where he would get himself lost. When he was totally back in that feeling of being lost the question came up in me: "*Who is watching all of this here?*". His immediate response was "*My mother*". Followed at once by "*... and I'm looking for my father*".

Using the technique I've just described above for resolving a double image, it was possible for the trainer to end up being able to clearly distinguish between a training situation and his mother.

Internally they were allowed to be seen to be different. Placing his father behind him gave him a lot more strength and he was able to quite easily look at the situation of being in a training, even while being in a state of 'not-knowing'. It does actually quite often happen that people feel the same way towards a (new) group as they do towards their own mother. If someone, such as this trainer, feels quite heavily judged by his or her mother, then he or she will equally feel judged by any group they happen to be in.

7.7 The work mid-life crisis

Around the age of forty some people have the feeling they need to go and do something completely different for a change. Unlikely inclinations suddenly seem to be presenting themselves as impossible urges that even the person him or herself cannot figure out. A perfect example of this happened to come up during a short workshop I was doing once.

A woman told me: "*I'm presently running my own private practice in the care sector. I want to work in the world of business, as a trainer. I have the capacities but something seems to be holding me back. To do this I'd be making a 180 degree turn about in my career*".

When the woman lined up representatives for her practice and for herself she placed both of them very close to each other. You could cut the tension between the two representatives with a knife. I started to get the sense that *"We're looking at a family issue here. Who is protecting whom?"*.

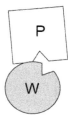

W = woman wanting to work in business world
P = present private practice

Then the representative of the woman herself turned away and took a few steps backwards. This was a big relief for her. The private practice representative said: *"This feels like goodbye".*

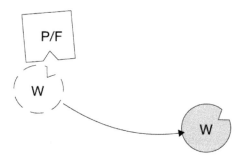

P/F = private practice, while also being the woman's father

It became obvious, from the way the representative for the private practice looked at the representative for the woman herself that the private practice was also representing the woman's father, although we were not actually mentioning this fact. The woman then said to her private practice: *"I'll leave this with you. I've a great deal to be grateful for to you"*. And then a bit later she continued: *"Please don't reject me if I decide to take on something new"*. Then, behind this woman, I set up her mother. There did not seem to be much strength there but when I placed the grandmother behind the woman's mother all three of them almost fell backwards. And it took placing yet another woman behind the grandmother, representing 'Eve', to have the female energy flowing forwards through all the women towards the client.

Then a representative for her 'new work' was set up in the constellation and the representative of this new work became very interested in the woman. The woman then said to her 'new work' *"If you could please hold on a bit longer and be patient I'll be available for you soon"*.

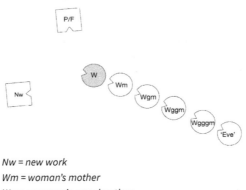

Nw = new work
Wm = woman's mother
Wgm = woman's grandmother
Wggm = woman's great-grandmother etc

While all this was going on the woman who had actually brought this issue to the workshop was radiant and, at the same time, deeply moved. There wasn't much need to say anything more. *"We don't need to know what was going on there in the family. The words you chose at the beginning were remarkable: you were talking about a 180 degree turn-about. Taking into account what we've seen here it looks like it would have something to do with turning from one parent to the other"*.

The inner process going on in a mid-life crisis, where the very parent who has been given less attention in the past by someone, is now taken closer to that person's heart, can also have a big impact on the work life of such a person.

7.8 Who are you honouring by doing it this way?

When you suspect that something of a family system is being played out at work it can help to bring out the magic question: *"Who are you 'granting honour to' by doing it in this way?"*. When this question is asked in all honesty, without wanting to change anything in any way, it can invoke a spontaneous answer such as: *"My grandmother"*. Such a response will very often also be a surprise, even for the person being asked. This happens because it is the system or 'soul' that is answering the question through the person speaking and the answer is not coming from the person's own individual awareness of what is happening. For this very reason it is difficult to ask yourself such a question. If you are asking yourself you will tend to be listening for an answer more cognitively and it will not be coming so much from the position of being in touch with the soul of the family system. Movement can happen if a friend or colleague asks the question for you. The system or the 'soul' (whichever image you prefer) will then carry the movement further.

Is there any way to imagine that you can avoid bringing something from your family background into your work? When you realise that, for you and also for all your colleagues, it is simply true that everybody brings something from their past and family system with them to work, it can give you the chance to see these people through different eyes and perhaps understand them a bit better. What is it we are talking about then when we talk about constellations?

About the method of system constellations

8

What is all this fuss, then, about constellations? Let's start by calling on Bert Hellinger to speak first. He developed this method from the experience he gained as both philosopher and therapist and has made it available to us.

How does your model work in the context of organisations?

Hellinger: *"To answer this I would first need to explain what exactly my model is. The model is derived from family constellations. In a family constellation someone will choose from the group present a few individuals to represent various members of his or her family. He then sets them up in the space in the middle of the group, in relation to one another. As soon as any one of these representatives has taken his or her position within the constellation they will start to take on the feelings of whomever it is they are representing, even though this representative has no actual knowledge about the person he or she is representing whatsoever. Using the constellation in this way helps us to form a clear picture of what is going on in the family system. If we then apply this same method to an organisation we can provide a useful overview of the organisation itself. We can gain a sense of how the members of the organisation are doing, as well as the state of health of other important elements of the organisation such as the departments, customers of the organisation etc."*

What does it mean to have a clear picture of what is going on?

Hellinger: *"Let's take the example of a man who is in the top management of an organisation and in a constellation he sets up representatives for his management team and also for himself. He would do all of this without thinking much about it. In a fairly short time he would start to get a clear picture of the relationships between himself and his managers.*

He might, for example, be surprised by seeing that some of the managers were turning away from him and turning towards something apparently outside the organisation itself. This might have been something he had not been aware of before setting up the constellation."

What do you mean when you talk about some of the people in the constellation turning towards something 'outside' the organisation instead of being turned towards him?

Hellinger: *"What I mean by saying this is that, in this example, some of the managers were not satisfied with what was going on in the organisation. It could, for instance, be that the top manager was using his authority in a way that was not supportive to his managers. This would make them feel unsettled and they would not feel free to give their full energy and intention to the organisation. If they happen to be able and competent managers they will be looking around for somewhere else to make their contribution, outside of this particular organisation."*

And then?

Hellinger: *"If we were to see something like this we would naturally be asking ourselves: what we could do to improve the situation? The constellation facilitator, one of whose roles it is to support the manager in setting up the constellation, would then propose certain steps that might be taken, within the constellation itself, as a way of looking for a workable solution for this situation for all involved."*

How?

Hellinger: *"The facilitator, for example, could turn the top manager to face towards the other managers and then have the managers face the top manager. It might also be the case that some of the managers are not positioned in the best place for them in the constellation. This might, for instance, be a situation in which a manager, who joined the organisation later than other managers, is attempting to place himself in the number one position within the management structure.*

This would irritate the other managers. The facilitator, in this case, might suggest having all the managers line up in a particular order within the constellation, according to how long they have been with the organisation, so that everyone feels they are standing in their right place."

Do those who are just observing the constellation also understand what the solution might be for the organisation or is it only confined to those who are acting as the representatives within the constellation itself?

Hellinger: *"Everyone who is watching the constellation, including the person who brought in the issue on which the constellation is based, will be able to see clearly in which positions within the constellation any representative feels comfortable. Because this work is done with representatives who have no present knowledge of the managers or the situation in the organisation, no-one can possibly influence what is happening in a constellation, not even some very ambitious colleague who might be wanting the constellation to show up something particular. The representatives in any constellation are simply reflecting what is actually going on in reality. Those who are actually involved in the real-life situation that is being portrayed in the constellation can, if they stay open, see what is really happening. Doing this can have profound effects because they will not be able to defend themselves against what they are seeing presented to them in the constellation. The mind is not really of much use in such a situation simply because it is the deeper truths of what is actually going that are being revealed. This is to say that organisation constellations can be used as powerful means to bring to light exactly what is going on in an organisation and thus, also, to suggest possible solutions to problems that the organisation may be suffering from."*

So far this has been Hellinger.

Difficult to believe? How does this all work then? What would have happened if different representatives had been chosen for a constellation? How much influence does the facilitator have on the whole affair? What is the theory behind all of this? These sorts of questions come up again and again, even in workshops in which consultants from a wide variety of different backgrounds are taking part. To be more precise these questions actually came from only two of the hundred or so participants in the workshops. The questions were asked by two quality control experts. They were struggling with themselves after watching their first constellation. Quite openly, and almost apologetically, one consultant said: *"I'm an engineer by background. For me 'to measure is to know'. So you can understand that I would find this sort of thing hard to swallow".*

Yes, it was for me too, as a scientist. I can manage things like 'the knowing field', which is much the same as the fields of gravity or the 'morphogenic fields' of Rupert Sheldrake. I can also compare this information with a model that comes from my own speciality – biology – where is it known that each individual cell carries knowledge of the bodily system as a whole, as a sort of holographically-stored information. Although it is unclear exactly how young cells in our body know what they should become, it seems that being at a particular point, for example, in the liver is enough information to stimulate the cells that happen to be there to become liver cells. I admit, however, that it is still only a model or even only an analogy that may be of help in accepting the phenomena that we are observing happening in constellations, over and over again. But such a model still does not provide us with a full explanation of why representatives feel and behave as they do when representing some of the elements of the real system. Actually I'm even more amazed by just how few questions people have when watching a constellation, and how many people just seem to accept these phenomena as being true. That is amazing. Perhaps there is some sort of 'primal knowing' going on here. Equally as strange is the fact that almost anyone can serve as a representative. Many representatives are astonished by the feelings they have when taking part in a constellation, just as I was, when I was a representative in my first constellation. In fact, even to this day, I'm newly surprised by the feeling every time I represent someone in a constellation.

But let's have an actual representative speak here: "*This is my first time as being part of an organisation constellation. I'm representing a young man, unknown to me, who is a project manager. I've no real idea what a project manager is or what is expected of me here. Around me others are fulfilling other roles: the principal manager, an employee in a particular project, someone representing 'the African-children-with-whom-this-project-is-concerned'. And several others whom I hardly remember who they are. In one way or another it is difficult to look at them. The constellation facilitator asked me to do something: I should look the principal manager directly in the eyes. I do not know this man, I have never met him before today. Actually I'm always a bit uncomfortable when I have to look at anyone in the eyes directly. But, O.K., I'll do it. Then something really strange happened. The moment I looked at the principal manager directly I felt I was better than him and I could feel myself becoming quite disdainful of this man. This is re-*

ally embarrassing. I mean only a minute ago he was sitting just two chairs away from me in the circle and he looked a regular sort of guy to me and now all of this starts happening. The facilitator asked me how I was doing. I felt uncomfortable about expressing, in front of the whole group, the fact that I was actually feeling a lot of disdain for the person representing the principal manager. And yet, something in me tells me that this is actually what is really going on, in reality, between the project manager and the principal manager. The real project manager, whose situation is being depicted here by this constellation, is sitting off to the side.

He watches me intently and nods, even confirming that the feelings that I am having are accurate. With this support I feel a little freer to be the representative. Later, when someone is lined up to be the Foreign Office of the Government, I'm amazed to feel my body turning away and beginning to collapse. I've got goose-pimples all up my arms and am freezing cold.

Similar things happened to me later, when playing different roles within these constellations. In fact, several times I was experiencing feelings that were new to me. There was one time when, totally unexpectedly, I felt tears burning my eyes. Is this about myself or about the one whom I am representing? In one way or another I discovered, during the course of the day, that it felt really good to me to be fulfilling these roles in constellations..."

Maybe, one day, there will be an explanation of how it is possible that people in a constellation can feel and act like the people they are representing. Not much is said in constellations. In the so-called 'masked constellations' nobody knows who he or she is representing, not even the facilitator. No-one knows either what sort of organisation it is, except, of course, the person whose issue is being presented in the constellation, who will obviously know who is representing whom. Using a masked constellation prevents the representatives, the observers and the facilitator from creating any pre-conceived ideas or prejudices about what is going on in the organisation, because nobody knows anything about what the constellation is all about. This way of working also does not allow the representatives to influence what is happening through their opinions or through knowing what the content is of the constellation. However, for the person who is bringing in the issue that is being considered, a masked constellation is just as powerful as one that it 'open', in which everyone knows what is going on.

When working with constellations, or with systemic work in general, we are working with a particular sort of information that comes from the fact that we belong to, or are being, part of a system. It is not information that is being communicated either verbally, on paper or in some mental way. The information we address in constellation work seems to be stored in our bodies in a more unconscious or subconscious way than the information we consciously know about the organization. This is the reason why we always ask the person who is setting up an organization constellation to get 'out of your head', and to set up the elements of the constellation in 'an intuitive way, that will allow you to be more led by your body than by your mind'.

In the field created in a constellation a representative will receive information about how a particular position within that field feels at that moment. They will have information about the relationship between that particular position, where they happen to be standing within the field, and other positions, or elements, in the system. They sometimes will also get a sense of which position within the field could be better for them. All this 'knowing' is coming despite having no spoken or written information about the function or person they happen to be representing, or about the organisation itself. It is not quite clear at the moment exactly how the information transfer process happens. Research done in Germany has shown that a representative's reactions to being placed in a certain position within a constellation are duplicable and valid. But this does not tell us anything more about how it all works. Luckily, more and more research is now being done about the phenomenon of constellations and the effects that constellations have on those participating in them.

As well as being a particular method, the work with constellations has also been described by Bert Hellinger as being a sort of 'phenomenological way of observing'.

He calls it 'phenomenological' because it makes the observation primary. It becomes about what you see in a system, person or constellation. Observing in this way is done without having opinions or judgements about what is being observed and without putting oneself above or below the other person, but while staying sensitively connected to the system as a whole. Undoubtedly, it is this 'inner attitude' that makes the phenomenon of the constellations so valuable. It is the attitude with which the facilitator approaches this work that allows constellations to bring essential truths to light that might otherwise never have been recognised. However simple the method of using constellations might seem to be, it is not something to ever be taken on lightly. It takes years of intense training in observation, having the appropriate attitude and sensitivity when working, and also a great deal of experience in how to facilitate a constellation, if this constellation work is to be done fruitfully. Fortunately the participants themselves can also tell, from the way a facilitator is working and the sphere that is being created, whether their particular issues are in good hands or not. The facilitator is not in charge in any way. He or she is a sort of host. He or she creates the circumstances in which something can be revealed for the person bringing up a particular issue and perhaps something can start to move forward in this area that was stuck before.

For what sorts of things can these constellations be used?

8.1 An outline of some of the possibilities

Organisation constellations can be helpful to clarify such questions as: *"What is going on in this situation, in this organisation or system?"* As such is can be a diagnostic instrument. Constellations can also work as an instrument of change. The constellation makes something happen in an organisation.

For example, the result of doing a constellation may be that a different organisational structure is found, wherein all the managers feel they have their place and can work together in harmony. Constellations can also be useful as a design instrument, or when creating possible scenarios. Different possibilities, or alternative developments of the organisation, can be tested out in a constellation. What would happen if this clinic took control of its own affairs? Would the patients feel better or worse if that were the case? How would customers respond to logo A and to logo B?

Here below I've listed a number of questions that organisational constellations may be able to provide answers for:

- Discovering and analysing bottle-necks in a structure
  Examples:
  - a department is being overloaded with too much work to be done by too few people,

- – Organisational structures that are not clear,
- – Boundaries between roles not well defined
- – Lack of, or insufficient, structures for coordination and communication
- Questions about leadership, like:
  - – How could the organisation become more decisive?
  - – How can more structure be brought to the management team
  - – Focus inward/outward
- Potential conflicts
- Behaviour patterns that are putting an organisation under undue pressure such as:
  - – Lack of respect
  - – Forming coalitions and territorial stand-offs
  - – Not keeping work and private affairs separate
  - – Arrogant behaviour, rebelliousness
  - – Positions or responsibilities not covered
  - – Black sheep
  - – High turnover of staff
- Re-focussing the organisation on achievable targets and realistic strategies
- Setting up an organisation or managing a merger
- Questions of who is to be the successor in a family business
- To investigate one's own position within an organisation
- To brief consultants:
  - – What is going on in the organisation I'm in charge of?
  - – What are the possibilities for my position within the organisation?
  - – How much am I, myself, trapped in the organisation?

- When needing to take decisions
    - Should I stay or leave?
    - Do we take on this challenge or let it pass?
    - Who of the applicants we have interviewed would best fit the position we have open?
    - Does this function need to be filled anyway?
- When looking for a good atmosphere in the work place:
    - Where might there be lack of support for a person or team?
    - In which position, and how, could someone's health be jeopardised? How can we prevent burn-out?
- Questions to do with marketing, products, customer relations
- Questions regarding a career

8.2 Can you use constellations for just about anything?

No, that is not possible. There are certain conditions and limitation that need to be taken into account when using constellations. A constellation will work well if the issue being brought for consideration by someone is actually something that really occupies that person. If someone is just doing a constellation out of idle curiosity it is almost as though the constellation starts to crumble and falls apart very rapidly. A constellation is not meant to relieve someone or some organisation of a particular task that has to be done or responsibility that must be assumed. A constellation also will not soften a harsh reality.

If someone has made up their minds, within themselves, to fire a particular employee, or to set up a merger of two departments, then a constellation will not make these processes any easier. A person will always have to bear the full consequences of any decision that person makes. Every step taken by someone along their path of growth and development involves, inherently, the need to deal with certain things and leave other things behind. Development and growth require exceeding the boundaries of one's conscience and, herein, lies power. Sometimes non-action, and prolonging the misery, seems easier than growing into the next step.

A constellation will not change this reality and that is why you should not set up a constellation if this dynamic is present in a situation. If a facilitator were to go along with a casual question from a client, and set up a constellation, the facilitator, in doing this, is actually taking over responsibility from the client. This weakens the client and diminishes his or her dignity. It also dis-empowers the facilitator in his or her role.

It also does not work if an employee wants to do a constellation as a way to change the management or to prove that he is right in a particular circumstance. By allowing this to happen the employee would end up feeling superior to his or her boss. On top of all of that the employee is in no way even able to change anything in an organisation. He doesn't have the position of the boss. All that is possible in any particular situation is to work just with the field: *"What, given my position within the system at present, is going on; and what can I, given where I am in the system, do here?"*. We do not do constellations that reach beyond someone's sphere of influence.

There are some magic words that can help a facilitator or client have insight into whether or not a constellation is a good idea in a particular situation. They are: *"Does this constellation, at this moment, strengthen or weaken the system as a whole?"*

Constellation work, however popular it might be becoming at the moment, is not a cure-all. It is neither a set of recipes for how to act or what to decide, nor should it be used as a way to make certain action seem legitimate or excusable. *"I went to a constellation and it became clear that I had to fire my business partner"* would turn constellations into being a sort of second-rate fortune-telling business. Constellations can provide very useful information to help someone in the process of making a particular decision. They often help by offering a different way of looking at a particular question and, by doing this, things become set in a new context. It would be going too far if you were to make yourself completely dependent on what a constellation shows. If this were allowed to happen the constellation would then take over and the person bringing question to the constellation would lose his or her responsibility and power. We would then be putting the cart before the horse.

Constellations can bring to light important information about an organisation, offering alternative possibilities in a given situation. What the client will then do with such information is totally up to that person. Real life is out there on the street or factory floor.

Can you send me your résumé?

9

What will empower someone in doing his or her particular job?

Which résumé do you mean – the normal, conventional one or the systemic résumé? What do you want to know about me? Graduated Cum Laude in Biology and later in Educational Sciences: teacher, manager with a multinational company providing technical support, organisational consultant and trainer and, lately, constellation facilitator. Is that what you would like to know? And as far as the last one goes – constellation facilitator – then I'm in the same boat as you and my young adult children when it comes to an explanation. My children regularly say to me: *"What do you want me to say when someone asks me what kind of work my father does?"*

Or do you want to know about me that, as long as I can remember, ever since being a toddler, I've had a deep respect for living systems? Do you want to hear that until the age of forty I was more of a mother's son (I could even potentially qualify to be the President of the 'Mother's Sons Society' – we all do have a number of interesting qualities in common). Would you like to know that in the last ten years much more of the force coming from my father and the father's side of my family system have become available to me? And what about knowing whether I have cut myself off from the work I did formerly and regard that as a lost part of my life, or whether that experience of my former work still acts as a source of inspiration for me and provides a basis for what I'm doing today? You might also want to be told that I am, systemically speaking, what could be called a 'Sunday child' and, therefore, have the tendency to give more than to take? Certainly part of what is important information to know about me would be that a great-grandfather of mine shot himself through the head on the Jangtse Kiang because he had failed. He had failed as a commander of a warship and I, therefore, will tend unconsciously to redeem a guilt and do something good for the world. Would you be interested to know that for me my family will always come first and my work will take second place? You might question whether this fact gives me more strength or makes me less available. If you've been trained to observe things from a systemic point of view, ladies and gentlemen of my future employer, I don't have to tell you much because you'll see it all at glance, perhaps confirmed with my answers to just one or two questions from you.

Maybe, dear employer, because you know, systemically speaking, what the job involves, your task would be to find out what sort of person you would need in this position and who would be the best person to do such a job.

9.1 The job opportunity

There was a large, multi-national package distribution company that dared to use constellations to fill a vacancy they had in this very same way. Firstly, a representative was set up for the vacancy in the team in which it was occurring, to make sure that there really was a position available there, from a systemic point of view. The boss, who had just recently seen three applicants for this position and their respective C.V.'s, set up, one at a time, three different representatives for each of the three applicants. He used the constellation as a source of extra information about what effect each of the applicants might have on the existing team. One of the applicants seemed to fit in with the team the best. On paper he did not seem to have a chance – too old, only five years before he was due to retire and a military background. When he came back for his second interview they were seeing him in a different light, they ended up hiring this man and it worked out just fine.

What seemed to happen was that not only did this particular man have a lot of positive energy about him, but he also brought a lot of equanimity to the team as whole, that was mostly comprised of young, ambitious people. No longer having a need to prove himself, he had an inner freedom and was thus much more autonomous. He enjoyed the work, and was happy to give a few more years of his positive energy to this company. He turned out to be someone who brought an element of stability and calm to how the team was organised.

Many people come to our workshops with questions about what should be the next step in their professional career. If you can open yourself up to such people you will often be able to sense how much personal power they have, if they would be an attractive proposition for an employer or for customers or if there, perhaps, is something that, at this moment, is lacking. Is a person ready and available to take on a new job or are they, in some way, still feeling connected to their previous job or to something else entirely different?

There is a particular strength and power to someone who has all his training, previous employment and everything to do with his professional background, as it were, behind him. This is the case even if this person has been on somewhat of a detour before arriving at where he or she is now. People sometimes want to go off in a completely different direction in their careers. Someone, say a managing director of a security company, wants to start up in spiritual practice, or a doctor practicing in general practice wants to get into practicing alternative medicine, a nurse wants to become a therapist, an astrologist fancies becoming a trainer in the business world, etc. etc. When taking such steps it makes a huge difference how you see your past. Are you able to honour and acknowledge what you have done in the past and lovingly see it as all part of yourself or do you reject what you've done up to now and consider it a wasted part of your life.

Imagine looking at the owner of a bookshop while knowing this man worked for many years as an engineer. If you can see his engineering background as something there behind him, supporting him, does this give him more or less strength?

By doing this you can check for yourself what place have you given all the things you've done in your past for work, inside yourself. You can, if need be, test this out in a simple way with the help of friends, who would be happy to assist you in something that is quite important for you. Without telling them who they are you can set them up as representatives of your former jobs. Then set yourself up in relation to all of them. You then can check how you feel in relation to each one of these jobs. Look at each person. Perhaps there is something that needs to be said or exchanged? Perhaps somewhere else feels better? It could even be that each representative, not knowing anything about what or who they represent, would like to say how they are feeling in that particular position.

Here is an example of how such a mini-constellation might work.

9.2 Intelligence work

A man who is due to become a partner in an organisation wanted to look at the role his former work and training had in his present work as a Gestalt teacher. He chose a representative for himself, one for the intelligence work he previously had done for the Police, one for the Gestalt and a representative for systemic work. Having selected these people he set them up in a constellation.

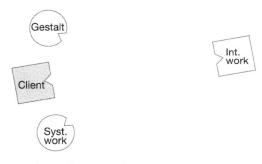

Int. work = Intellegence work
Syst. work = Systemic work

The representative for the Gestalt looked at the representative of the intelligence work and was immediately overcome with deep grief. At that moment I invited the teacher, who had asked the question, to take up the position in the constellation himself and I continued to work with him directly in this way. I suspected that there was something here that was incomplete and needed to be completed. The teacher looked at the representative of his work as a police officer and after a long while he took two steps towards this person and they lovingly embraced.

The representative for systemic work, who felt restless and not in her right place, was given a position on the other side of the Gestalt. The representative of Gestalt, who had not had the feeling up to that point of having been seen, came much more to rest. After another moment the intelligence work representative stood behind the teacher, the representatives for the Gestalt and the systemic work held hands and slid up closer to the teacher. The teacher felt calm and the other representatives felt a calmer, quieter strength.

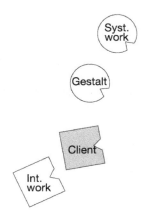

The teacher told us later that he still could see his father behind the intelligence work he had done with the Police. Both his mother and father had been in the Resistance during the War, where his father had done intelligence work. The grief and guilt that the teacher felt about the fact that he had abandoned the intelligence work disappeared during the constellation and changed into a supportive force. The teacher said: *"This intelligence work represented both security and risk. I often used to take considerable risks in that work, just as my father had done previously during the War"*.

We can see here how children can be bound up in the fate and work of their parents through the work they choose to do. Sometimes children will take on the huge job of trying to complete something that their parents were not able to bring to an end. Imagine the pain then if you decide to leave such a profession behind and the ensuing guilt that can be experienced in so doing. Going back to our example constellation – the son could see his father, in the guise of the representative for police intelligence work, looking at him in such a way now that reconciliation, and an inner sense of peace and strength, became possible for the son. The son, in fact, was now able to actually receive his father's strength, without needing to fulfil his father's unfinished business from the War.

9.3 Some sort of order of previous work experiences

What we could also see in this constellation is that arranging previous work experiences and vocational training in a certain way, can bring
feelings of peace and of coming to rest for someone. In our example the
representative for Systemic Work felt restless and not in her rightful place
when positioned close to the teacher on the teacher's right-hand side. It
was only when she was moved to the behind and left of the Gestalt, that
the representative of Systemic Work, felt seen and valued again. Both representatives then both spontaneously joined hands. The latter position
acknowledges that Gestalt was there before Systemic Work.

We often notice that when someone starts up something new that they
put this new project in first place, systemically speaking. In constellations
we see that, if this is the case, then the representatives for the work experience and education that made it possible for that person to be where he
is now in his career, become restless, and they don't feel they have been
properly honoured for what they are. What we also see in these constellations is that the most recent training that a person has done does not
feel, in any way, the need to topple previous trainings from their positions
higher up in the system's order. Rather, they feel quite content to go to
the back of the queue. Sometimes we see what looks like coalitions being
formed between more recent training and earlier trainings in cases where
those previous trainings have not been fully acknowledged and honoured.
With such a coalition in place it is not possible to gain the full benefits of
the later training, which can only really happen when the earlier trainings
have been given their due respect.

New beginnings, a new job, or setting up a new department in an organisation, obviously require care and attention.

They all need some sort of protection in order to get properly established. But, as soon as whatever is new is out of its nappies and is able to
stand on its own two feet, it is a good idea to take another look at where
this new shoot that is sprouting should fit into the system as a whole. If
new undertakings end up being put above whatever came before, and the
previous experiences and achievements are, thereby, not properly valued
and honoured, then the position taken by these latest developments will
end up with problems and there is a much greater chance of conflicts of

one sort or another developing.

For example, if you have a situation where there is a company that is committed to growth, but that does not fully respect and honour those of its employees who have been with the company the longest, then those who are recruited later into the company will be unsure and will be asking themselves: *"Is it OK to grow here?"* Therapists who are enthusiastic about systemic work may tend to put down other sorts of therapies. In the field of psycho-therapy at least, last century belonged to Freud, not to Bert Hellinger. Freud comes first in this case, then many others and perhaps Bert Hellinger is there is 87th place! Imagine how Hellinger would end up if he were to be placed ahead of Freud.

Every profession has its own great masters, who have brought that profession to where it is now and who are followed by others, who then can develop the expertise in that particular field further. The new direction that is taken may involve a 90° angle, but despite this fact, the new direction would not even have been possible if the previous work had not already been done.

A particular profession can develop further only if it is exposed to contradictions, antitheses, new observations and even criticism and, in fact, especially criticism.

If those who have come before are honoured as being part of any development that is presently under way, and maybe even as the only possible way that development can occur, then this will support and empower whatever comes later.

If criticism leads only to rejection of what has been recognised as being an important part of a particular field of work, or shame about it, or even the trying to hide it in some way, then all you end up with is being cut off from the roots of the profession itself. Customers are, by the way, extremely sensitive to whether or not something is connected with its roots.

OK, but how on earth do you put that down in your résumé?

9.4 Fulfilling someone else's dream

What should I put down in my résumé about my particular qualities? Probably all I'll put down is that I have them. I don't think I'll mention that I contribute these in honour of someone else. This sort of background is something I'll cherish but keep quiet about. At the end of a day of constellations, when we are almost out of time, a woman brought in an issue about her not being able to find her strength in the work that she is doing. The same appears to hold true for her father, a sister and a brother.

Facilitator *to woman*: *"Who are you honouring by not succeeding at work?"*

Tears came to this woman's eyes as she replied, instantly: *"My grandfather. He was a genius and he had difficult relating to people. We actually did not talk about him."* Then she set up her grandfather and immediately, herself, facing him.

The grandfather and the woman, his grand-daughter, looked at each other for a long time.

Facilitator *to woman*: *"Say to him: "Dear grandpa, I won't do better than you did.""*

Woman: *"Dear grandpa, I won't do better than you did".*

Facilitator *to woman*: *"Say to him: "Dear grandpa, I see you are connected to something else and are in contact with something else"".*

Woman: *"I see you are in contact with something else."*

The representative of the grandfather is beaming broadly.

Facilitator *to the group*: *"Previously they called it a 'contact disorder', but here you can see he is just in contact with something else."*

Facilitator *to woman*: *"This would be a good reason to do something in the field of contact with people. You would be honouring your grandfather by doing this."*

Facilitator *to group*: *"... And at the same time this act of honouring the grandfather will be doomed to failure, as long as the grand-daughter is thinking to herself that she will be helping her grandfather by not ever doing any better than he was able to do. As soon as the grandfather began smil-*

ing so broadly the grand-daughter understood that she cannot help him and that it would be quite alright for the grandfather if the grand-daughter were to succeed at her work."

We see a dynamic occurring in the present in this situation that happens frequently. A double loyalty exists to a person who is excluded from a system.

On the one hand the child or grand-child tries to realise the dream that someone else could not realise, while, at the same time, knowing that any attempts to do this are bound to fail. The reason for this is that, trying to save someone or honour someone, she inevitably places herself, systemically, above the parent or grand-parent she is trying to rescue or honour. This is how it ends up as a double-bind: Whatever the child does, succeeding at work or not, will in both cases be associated with feelings of guilt.

If, for instance, in a coaching situation, you would say to someone that it is not useful to repeat what grandpa did, then the client will only tend to get even more involved in a conflict of loyalties. If she were to accept the advice from the coach it might bring some temporary relief and she would be able to act. But after a while the hidden loyalty to the grandfather would make itself felt again. The grand-child succeeds in failing once again and thereby feels even more guilty. The solution to all of this is for the grand-daughter to be able to see the grandfather carrying the weight of his own fate and that he approves of his grand-daughter's going her own way. Having this happen the grand-daughter's previously blind, childish love and loyalty can be transferred over into a mature and conscious love. She can then stay connected with her grandfather and be free to fulfil what she needs to do in her own way, by succeeding in her work. She turns herself, internally, towards the future. Her grandfather can stand behind her and becomes a sort of 'patron saint' for her. Also, for that matter, the woman came up after the workshop and said: *"That is exactly what I want to do – to become a communications trainer".*

9.5 Being in service to something

Sometimes people are 'taken into service' by something larger - a larger system such as a country or nation. This may put someone in a modest position or an elevated position. Nevertheless, it will always be without that person consciously wanting this or knowing about it. It seems that the system more or less arbitrarily chooses people to put right something that has gone awry in the past. In such a situation it is difficult to have any real opinions about what might be happening.

These are obviously far-reaching observations and thoughts. We don't know how it actually works and perhaps we should just let it be so. That being the case, here are a few examples from the past:

A woman from Suriname, living and working in Nederland, has the on-going feeling that her life's work is to do something in Suriname, without knowing exactly what that might be. Every time the subject gets mentioned she is very moved. The training and work she is doing in the Nederlands are not easy. They are more like way-stations or preparations for something else. It is not that she has some goal, but rather the goal has her. She is modest whenever talking about it, not making much of herself.

A young and energetic Dutch woman, working in a government ministry, is trying to find her right place in the organisation. She suffers from the fact that she tends to look down on her colleagues. It seems that she, somehow, has a connection with 'the fate of the world'. This tends to set her above her colleagues, which ends up with them not being too happy with her.

A Dutch person is attending a large, international conference about war and peace. An Israeli and a Palestinian give a lecture together. The Palestinian recounts how he had grown up on the West Bank and how for his whole life he had known nothing but throwing stones at Israeli soldiers and tanks. He continued to speak about how, when he was captured and thrown into prison in the Negev desert, that he saw all his Israeli guards as being identical to each other and as representatives of the very people he hated so much.

It was only months later, when two Israeli guards got into a quarrel about a request that the Palestinian had made to be given a sip of water, that he began to see that every Israeli guard was different. At that moment, for him, they changed from being 'the enemy' to being people.

From that moment on everything changed. The Israeli told about his being a descendant of the Holocaust victims and that in the '70's he had started to wonder what had happened to the descendants of the Nazi murderers. That began a very slow process that ended up, a few years later, in the meeting together of a group of 17 descendants from the Holocaust victims with 18 descendants of Nazi murderers. They began with a round of everyone telling a bit about him- or herself.

They had agreed to take two days to do this, but, in fact, it ended up lasting for three and a half days before everyone had been able to speak. It was clear that they felt very closely bonded to each other and will certainly meet again in a year's time.

When they came back together again the next year, many are in low-spirits. It turns out that during that last year, when they had returned to their home countries and had spoken about what had happened in their meeting together, it was very difficult for them to be accepted back in to their own groups. They were judged as being guilty.

At the end of the lecture it turned out that Martin Bohrmann, the son of Martin Bohrmann, Hitler's secretary, was also at this conference and that he would be giving a lecture in an hour.

The Dutchman felt inexplicably drawn to attend this lecture, even though he had not originally planned to do so. He quickly changed his programme and arrived in the auditorium where the lecture had begun just a few minutes late.

Martin Bohrmann was sitting behind a table, telling his story. He had been a boy at a special school for the high-up Nazis in Munich, had later moved to Berchtesgraden and, finally, when it was known that the war was lost, he was posted as soldier to Southern Tyrol. He was telling this story in a very matter-of-fact way, how it all went, without making it any better or worse than it was. You could have heard a pin drop in the auditorium. As Martin Bohrmann was speaking about the moment when he had realised what this man, who to him had been a loving father and husband, had also done, as the secretary of Hitler, the despair on his face had made a profound impression on the Dutchman listening to this lecture. The expression at that moment on Martin Bohrmann's face was deeply imprinted in the Dutchman's memory. Bohrmann later became a Catholic priest and has, for many years, been involved in peace education in schools all over Germany. The Dutchman, sitting on the floor in the over-crowded auditorium, listened in complete silence, as tears streamed down his face, without his knowing why. He felt as though a strong, invisible hand was guiding him and giving him such a strong urge to go over to Martin Bohrmann.

During a short intermission he got up and walked over. Martin Bohr-mann also rose and, on seeing the Dutchman's tear-streaked face said: *"Oh dear, what is happening with you?"* The Dutchman, could not hold back his tears any longer. As though guided by some external force, he laid his head on Borhmann's shoulder and said: *"I come from Holland, and it is May 4th today, the day we commemorate our dead..."*.

After the break, when Borhmann continued to give his lecture and there was an opportunity to ask questions, the Dutchman felt, strangely enough, an enormous sense of deeper peace and coming to rest.

Looking back, he often wonders what it was that happened at that con-ference. He has no connection with victims of the Holocaust in his own background and is not even Jewish. It felt just as though he was a repre-sentative in a constellation, as though he was serving something larger. And that is just how he left it.

Products are just like human beings

10

How does a new product, concept or direction in our work, end up being successful?

When someone said to me that he wanted to do his PhD thesis on the subject of constellations about product branding I was interested. Or should we say I was totally fascinated by the idea. Would the systemic vision and method of doing constellations, that had been developed from a vision about profound human questions, be useable for something as purely economically-driven as a marketing strategty or branding issues? We had already seen that setting up products or logos in constellations could provide useful insights. But how would this be to research all of this in a systematic and scientific way? I was especially moved by the courage of the researcher, who was willing to do a scientific investigation into something so incomprehensible and elusive as a constellation. He was willing to let two worlds nakedly face each other. The fact he was prepared to spend four years of his life doing this, risking losing his scientific credibility in the scientific world and thus putting his whole career on the line, certainly gained my respect.

To my greatest surprise it appeared that the constellation approach was interesting for not only brand managers (just the name implies immediately that a brand makes up an essential element in the system of an organisation) but also for marketing gurus and experts in the field of branding. Not just the method of constellations, but the whole systemic approach, is what seemed to make it interesting for them all. Questions of branding inevitably have to do with the relationships between a brand, a product, the manufacturers and the buyers of the product.

Constellations are an excellent way to create images for these relationships and to do research into them themselves. When people are asked, through questionnaires, to say what they think about a particular brand, and if they would buy such and such a new product, it turns out that, very often, what people actually do, does not match up with the answers they have previously given.

Brand managers are, therefore, always on the look out for new ways to get a better grip on what is going on in these relationships. How would a constellation focussed around a branding issue go? Here are some examples:

10.1 Baby food

A brand manager wanted to introduce an existing product to a new target group. He wanted to find out to what extent a new promotional campaign would reach this target group. *"The present advertising campaign
extols motherhood and particularly highlights the 'pink cloud' women tend
to experience around motherhood. This is especially successful during preg-
nancy"*, the brand manager said. *"But, as soon as the child is born the pink
cloud evaporates. Mothers are then faced with unexpected things happening that are not at all pleasant and beautiful. That is why we want to introduce a campaign that has a different tone – one that fits more accurately
with women's real experience after the baby is born. Will this proposed new
advertising campaign succeed in strengthening the emotional connection
between the target group and the product?"*.

Firstly the present situation is set up in a constellation so that, later on,
the consequences of introducing the new target group and new advertising campaign into the system, can be assessed.

The current situation is set up using representatives for, among others, the board of directors and the product (baby food). The moment the
product is set up he feels wobbly. The facilitator then asked if there had
ever been anything special about this product. Had there perhaps been
customers who had been negatively affected in any way by using the product. The brand manager said he had only been working with this company
for a couple of years, so did not know of anything prior to that time. Because there is a lack of actual information we set up a representative for
those who may have been harmed in some way by use of the product. We
chose a woman to be the representative. It was immediately apparent to
the representatives of the product and the representative for the 'harmed
persons' what was going on. The 'harmed persons' was a mother, whose
children had become ill from use of a defective product. However, the
mothers do not seem to bothered by it all. They simply say that they and
their children are now fine and are all now grown up. They just ask for
some truthfulness and, moreover, are full of confidence in the strength of
the product. If the former managers of the company producing the sub-
standard product could just admit that and be 'sincerely apologetic about
the fact that they had not foreseen what could have, and did happen', then
energy would start to flow back to the product. The representative for the

product felt that the incident had been 'blown out of all proportion' and is now ready to take-off.

In the follow up of this constellation the representative of the new target group had an uncomfortable feeling that she was putting herself forward at the expense of the older target group. She felt better in her position next to the old target group and, being there, she felt also recognised more by the management. The new campaign then feels connected up with the old campaign and the new target group, but not with the product. The new target group, for its part, would like a stronger product. *"You could almost go on to think of having a product split here"* commented the facilitator.

Later the brand manager watched a video of the constellation with two other directors from the company, who had not been able to be present at the original constellation workshop. These directors remarked at how much they were able to recognise the dynamics portrayed in the constellation and the reactions that they saw in the representatives. They also volunteered the information that the video had given them a whole new set of insights and useful information about the relationship between the brand and the new advertising campaign. And, not least of all, it appeared that there had actually been a group of customers who had been negatively affected by using the product. At some point there had been a fault in the production of the product and a whole batch of product had to be recalled.

10.2 Wha is going on inside repeats itself on the outside

What we have seen so far is that the relationship between a product and the market, or between a brand and a target customer group, will often mirror whatever the dynamics are that exist inside an organisation. When there is any tension inside an organisation it will be reflected in the relationship between a product and its customers. The relationship between a product and its customers will only be healed when the organisation has handled its own internal business.

Who doesn't recognize, from personal experience, the phenomenon of customers drawing away from you in those periods when you are unsettled and you are thus tending to be more inward-turned? As soon as you are back to full strength, available and outwardly directed in your attention, the customers start calling you up again! You could ask yourself: are the outside world and potential customers an integral part of your professional system?

Or are they somehow separated out from it? Equally, when you use your clients to solve something in your personal life, you run the risk of losing them permanently.

10.3 The hidden stakeholders

A large organisation, concerned with protecting wildlife and nature, wanted to develop a more 'modern' image for itself. They also wanted to attract more of the modern-day family types into their nature reserves, and not just the real die-hard nature-lovers, their present customers. There were designs submitted for new logos, a new colour scheme and new typeface. So we set up representatives for, among others, the present brand, the new brand, the present target group and the new target group and the decision makers. It became clear from the constellation that it would be impossible to just throw out the old brand image. The present target group does not agree with the new proposals. Change is only going to be possible when this older target group, that has supported the organisation for many years, feels acknowledged and treated with some sort of courtesy. They behave within the system as though they are the hidden stakeholders and owners of the organisation.

We see, more often, this sort of thing happening - where a brand becomes well known and trusted and almost public property in a way. There is just no way you can afford to mess around with such a brand. Such a brand works like a cog in the wheel of relationships between different elements of the system of the organisation. There are the relationships between products and the company, between product and target group, between target group and company and between several departments within the company – like the franchiser and franchisee.

Often you will have the impression that the brand acts as a sort of conscience for what is going on in a company and would be able to indicate which developments have a chance of succeeding and which have little power behind them. In this sense brands are significant elements to be taken into account in any system. I must confess that I do approach them differently now and give them more weight than I used to do.

10.4 A choice between two markets

A man had a Jungian therapy practice and was finding he was getting less and less clients. At one point he was offered work counselling the bereaved. He hesitated on making a commitment to this offer and wanted to know what would best for him to do. Added to all of this, he needed, fairly urgently, to earn more income to support his family. He mentioned that his current clients mostly come to him via referrals from two G.P.'s and two psychologists. In dialogue with the therapist we set up representatives for: the man, his present practice, then a representative for Jung, followed by three people sending him referrals (psychologists, doctors) and finally a client.

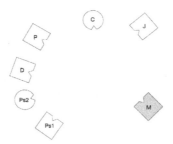

M = man with the issue about his most appropriate work
P = Practice, J = Jung
Ps1 = psychologists 1, Ps2 = psychologists 2
D = doctor, C = Client

In the constellation there was not one moment when the representative for the therapist himself was in contact with the others. Everything seemed heavy and apathetic. When the psychologists and doctor are set up they feel very unstable. Psychologists 1 looks down at the floor, and almost falls over. Psychologists 2 looks at Jung and wants to move backwards. The doctor wants to leave the constellation and lash out at those around him. The client stands there petulantly.

Then as the facilitator of the constellation, I turn the representative of the therapist around, to face away from all the others. Whereupon everyone starts to feel better immediately. Then I set up someone in front of the therapist.

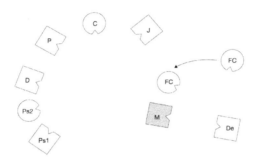

De = death
FC = future potential client

The representative I set up was death. A possible future client, who was also set up in the constellation, immediately feels at home. The future client feels even better when he is standing next to the therapist and looking at death together. The old client responds to this with relief: *"Finally it's clear that it's about death here"*. I muse out loud: *"Strange that first the therapist had a practice to do with life matters and here we see the work is done in the service of death"*. Therapist: *"Yes, when death was set up, I thought at first it was my father, who died a couple of years ago. It's correct. Ever since he passed away a great deal has changed for me"*. This constellation shows how different types of work fit the different phases of our lives. Here, also, we can again see how closely clients will respond to dynamics that are at play in a therapist's own system.

10.5 The title

As a publisher I was having trouble finding the appropriate title for a Dutch translation of one of Bert Hellinger's books. The German Title 'Die Quelle braucht nicht nach dem Weg zu fragen' (the Spring does not have to ask the way). The translator team, for the last six months, has already been using 'The Spring' as a working title, so it was tempting to take this over as the title. In the e-mail brainstorming sessions about the title, heated discussions were getting under way. *"Bert Hellinger does not want to be seen as the source. The book is not about the spring itself, but about what flows through the spring and finds its way"*. Added to all of this a branding expert was commenting that 'spring' has too many associations with German or mountain landscapes and that it would be good to find something that can be more associated with a Dutch landscape. In short, the usual procedure for finding a title, of brain-storming sessions that focus in more and more in a particular direction and ending up with a really powerful title, did not happen this time.

So I bring this question of the title into a constellation. It is common practice when doing branding constellations to bring in a particular design question, whereby several alternatives can be tested and the target group is set up to gauge their responses to the various alternatives. In this case we could try to test out three alternative titles for the book on the present target group (those people already familiar with Hellinger's systemic work) and perhaps on a target group seen in the future (those people for whom this book would be their first introduction to systemic work).

But there was also something else that was puzzling me here: I have the feeling that whatever I do I cannot make an appropriate choice at the moment, even if the constellation were to indicate one of the titles as being the favourite. Perhaps it was because there were already too many people involved in trying to resolve this question of the title. Perhaps I've given up too much control here or am trying to please too many people.

So I put a different question to myself: *"How do I end up being in a more decisive state myself, relative to the title of this book?"* There are already a number of titles to choose from but, what is puzzling me, is why I remain so indecisive about it all.

We set up: representatives for the book, Bert Hellinger and for the publisher. My question implies that it is not necessary, in the first place, to set up a representative for a target group as a reference point. In this case the publisher is acting as that.

The book, Bert Hellinger and the publisher are standing in a triangle. The book and the publisher slowly turn to face each other. 'Bert Hellinger' chuckles and says he does not want to interfere with the name but is happy to watch. The book and publisher look at each other for a long time and seem to grow in strength. Then I take the place of the person representing me as the publisher in the constellation. Standing in this particular position within the constellation I feel full of energy and the book is very attractive. I feel a certain sparkle in me and feel like getting the book finished fast, so that it can be printed. Strangely, standing there in the constellation, I was not worried too much about the fact that I couldn't immediately come up with a title. I took in the image of the constellation once more and then the short constellation was brought to an end.

The following morning I was busy doing the last corrections to the book and was, therefore, reading through and concentrating on the whole translation. At one moment a particular sentence caught my eye and I scribbled it down on a scrap paper that was next to me.

Half an hour later I realised, with great surprise: *"Hey, I've just written down the title for the book!"*. It was crystal clear to me, at once, that this was, in fact, the title. There was also no need for more consideration and testing it out on others. What was more: the colour scheme for the cover of the book was also suddenly clear and obvious to me. It turned out to be the same colour as the colour of the shirt worn by the representative of the book in the constellation the previous day. Instantly I also knew that the picture on the cover could be that of a Dutch landscape. The colours of the Dutch edition anyway were completely different from those of the German edition and also different from the cover design I had envisioned up to that point. It is still good to hear from people how much they like the cover of the book.

When someone, or a company, needs to make choices about products or how they should look or how they can be presented, it can be helpful to ask the opinion of others and this can bring up useful information. Similarly, a constellation can provide useful information, but there is also a risk involved in doing this. If an organisation is not already in a decisive mood, or cannot carry out a decision, then it is not very much use just to test out alternative scenarios. If such an enquiry, questionnaire or constellation simply replaces the organisation's own decision, taking away something of their own responsibility, it could end up weakening those who are involved in having to make the decisions. In such a situation it is much better if the company, or person involved, can first, themselves, become more decisive and then the decision will follow on naturally by itself.

10.6 Results from doing constellations on branding issues

Following on from the previously mentioned Ph.D. research on using constellations with company brands, five brand managers and consultants reported back on how things had gone after working with constellations. They also gave their impressions of how constellations could be applied in their line of work. All five of them had brought in a particular issue 6 to 12 months previously. For most of these managers the constellation approach was completely new. Since both their overall responses, and the way they talked about their experiences, were quite surprising, I'd like to quote them here directly.

The first marketing manager had an issue about a great, nationally recognised brand. The question had been: *"Would it be possible to introduce a new, sub-brand next to the existing brand"*. The top executive of this company had his own ideas about this matter and was being advised by the marketing manager. *"The emotional aspect was very surprising for me"*, he said. *"We tend to think we are very rational, but it was clear that emotional factors are also involved. And, what was made very clear in the constellation, was that these emotions were mainly connected to power issues within the company. The particular benefits I gained from doing the constellation were that I began to ask myself very different questions about the brand. Questions that I would never otherwise have come up with on my own. It was as though I was thinking in a completely different way, like being in a fourth dimension: looking from the outside at a situation that you are very personally involved in, and where you feel directly responsible and where there is also a very large company involved too.*

I see two fields where constellations could be applied in my particular pro-fession: firstly in the phase before we take decisions or, for example, give an advertising agency a particular account to work on. From the quality research available through a constellation I can see more clearly what el-ements are involved, what outside factors are playing a role and which of these are fundamental to the whole consideration. It is particularly relevant that we often see in these constellations that internal issues within a com-pany are playing a role in the decision making about a brand. Secondly I can see constellations being very useful to use in the whole process of creating different scenarios. The critical question for me is to what extent the choice of representatives and their responses in a constellation can be influenced by subjectivity. And just to add, the constellation we did gave weight to the decision not to introduce a sub-brand in our company."

The second marketing manager worked at a family business producing alcoholic beverages. They had had a question about what effect would introducing a new product have to their brand image and to the present target group of customers.

"The constellation gave me many insights into what sort of process to fol-low, but also a lot of information about how our brand, product and target group relate to each other. It also made me very aware of my own position in this company. My boss is a fourth-generation owner of this family busi-ness, that has been in existence for 115 years. I've been working here for two years and the constellation helped me be sensitive to the 113 years of business that had gone on before I arrived on the scene. Having done the constellation I'm not seeing him so much as my boss any more, but more as the 'field' in which I work. In fact I'm managing him! I think the greatest advantage I gained from doing constellations is that you can not only take a look at what is going on at the moment, but also how it was, and how it could be in the future. Most marketing research just looks at the present mo-ment. Using constellations allows you to test out possible changes.

A second advantage of constellations is that it provides the opportunity to feel into all the crucial elements in any situation – not just the market, competitors and target groups, but also what is going on within the com-pany itself".

The third manager is managing director of an IT company. He did a constellation with one of his co-managers and they had more of a strategic question: *"What effect will it have for us if we, working with the top 200 Dutch companies, also start to focus on the top range of small and mid-sized businesses? The constellation supported us in our plan to continue the path we had already set out on and we even accelerated somewhat down that course, just before the market collapsed. But the constellation held two more eye-openers for us. One of these was that it would be better if the founder, who is also a co-director, had more of a strategic, rather than operational, role in the company, and would thus be operating more in the background. We have had these changes in place for about six months. It happened very harmoniously and has worked out very positively for every-one involved and we are still gaining the benefits from this change that we made. The second eye-opener was that the customers of different customer groups did not see one another in the constellation. What we then did, hav-ing recognised that this was so, was to contact our customer groups and put them in touch with each other so that they could learn from each other. This works very well. We didn't say much in the board meetings about the con-stellation, but just got on and started doing things. From our point of view constellations are helpful in the process of change. You can make particular tensions, that might be present in a company, visible and thus start to do something constructive with these. What the constellation brought for me personally is that I trust my feelings and intuition more. Remarkably enough the idea of trusting one's intuition became a much more acceptable way of making decisions amongst the board of directors".*

The fourth brand expert works as a consultant for an organisation that manages a large part of the nature reserves in the Netherlands. *"The client who did the constellation was very moved by what happened. A lot hap-pened as regards the content of the question we had brought. We had want-ed to know how we could serve not just the old target group of customers but also draw more young, modern-day families out into nature. It helped us a great deal, when making all kinds of decisions, to see that it is really important for us not to exclude the older target group. We were also helped by this insight when it came to negotiating with suppliers of equipment and facilities about what would be installed in the nature reserves themselves".*

The fifth manager was a brand consultant. *"This method is useful in the whole process - from the very first decision to the last. The one condition, however, for using this approach is that you are willing to take a wider per-*

spective than just the actual project you are working on itself. Apart from this, it seems that the constellations are very helpful to me when you get stuck with something and want to take a look at what is going on. It also seems useful for an initial stock-take, when you are starting to consider a particular question such as: what is the present situation and what do we have to take into account? The method works fast and allows for openness. In fact, I feel it is necessary that the constellation is conducted in a positive atmosphere, where openness is permitted. During a constellation a kind of collective intelligence is at work to solve complex questions that are often too complicated to be resolved with the normal analytical thinking".

Without presenting the complete reports from these managers I was, and still am, genuinely impressed by the often far-reaching results and contributions that the constellations were able to produce when critical business decisions were being made.

What particularly stands out for me from these reports is that three of the five managers mentioned that constellations were not only helpful in regard to the presented issue, but beyond, that they had influenced their way of thinking about themselves or their organisations. I had never heard that sort of promising effect of using constellations so clearly expressed before.

A systemic test for road-worthiness

11

Someone who sat on the boards of three foundations, in the area of health care, wanted to have a sort of systemic M.O.T. [1] test for these three foundations. Her question was: *"I want to see if my three foundations are healthy and if there are points within these three that deserve my particular attention"*. These, and many other similar questions, are not because there is a problem in an organisation or at work. They are more coming from an underlying question such as: *"How do I manage my business best?" "What can I, as manager, add, from a systemic point of view, to what I am already doing?" "What is needing my attention at the moment in the development of this organisation?"* Or: *"When do organisations, and those working in organisation, function well, as seen from the systemic perspective?"*

As a kind of short summary of this book, we can highlight here a few key points. The following three systemic principles are valid, in order of importance:

Most importantly, there needs to be a clear structure within which the organisation, its departments, and every person working there, can function well.

Secondly, the balance between give and take is important. Without a proper balance of give and take no real exchanges are possible between the various elements of a system.

Lastly, people, ideals and other elements that have made their mark on the organisation in the past, should be given an appropriate place. They form the roots of the organisation. What also holds true for all employees is that each person has an equal right to a place within the organisation.

When we keep our attention on these principles a sort of 'meta-structure' begins to emerge for an organisation, that allows the work and the people in that organisation to thrive.

Remarkably the sequence of importance of these principles, when applied to family constellations, is different: There the most important principle is that everyone in a family system has a right to a place. Then comes having a clear structure within the family, followed by the balance of give and take. But, after all, an organisation does have a different function than a family and requires a different strength in order to be successful.

[1] the abbreviation standing for Ministry of Transport, used to refer to the British road-worthiness check-ups needed for cars older than three years

11.1 Order: a reliable place for everyone

If there is a place for everyone that they can trust, and a clear order to everything, then people do not have to concern themselves too much with questions about where, exactly, their true place is in the system, or the position of their colleagues or their boss. When the systemic structure is clear no-one needs to be bothered by such questions. This, in turn, means that everyone can concentrate on his or her work and employees are not interfering with each other's performance.

You can easily recognize an organization where this kind of order is met: There is a kind of calm present in the organisation. Managers who are not able to make a real contribution to creating and maintaining a clear systemic structure, will tend to create obstructions for any progress. They end up dis-empowering the organisation. This means that the only positions that should be maintained in that organisation are those that are really necessary for the system of that organisation to function effectively.

The same would hold true for a whole department or even a whole organisation. Does the society have a structure such that a particular organisation is given a viable place within it? While working in Croatia with a number of constellations in hospitals, in organisations set up for the rebuilding of the social structure there, and with technical companies, it became very evident just how much the uncertainties in both politics, and the society as a whole, were influencing these organisations. This was not just due to their being dependent on the decisions of government ministers. Seen from only this perspective you might be led to believe that the managers in these organisations were afraid or simply servile to higher authorities. But this was not actually the case. It was simply that the instabilities within the society were not allowing any structure to be provided within which these organisations could find a clear place for themselves in which they could function effectively.

It was, for that matter also, remarkable how many young people in Croatia were wanting to leave the country. Previously I might have thought that this would have been due to getting a better perspective on the balance of give and take. But when talking with these young people it was clear that it was much more to do with wanting a structure within which to work and wanting to find some rest. One of these young people gave me a business card with her name, address, country and then, in capitals, EUROPE. Flying back on the plane from Zagreb I realised just how self-evident is has become for me that, in the Netherlands, all the larger social frameworks are so stable. Despite all the little quarrels that come up here and there, and the occasional recession that can affect many people personally, the long-term, overall stability in the Netherlands is a blessing.

This idea filled me with a certain gratitude, including gratitude to all those who have contributed to this stability. If people cannot find a structure or reference points within an organisation where they are working, they will start looking for reference points within themselves. Such reference points may be their training background or their particular set of skills. These will be what they use to look for work – either within the job market of their country or abroad. If an organisation has many people with such 'internal' frames of reference you might suddenly find that their bonds with the organisation itself begin to fall away. What you then end up with is a collection of individual contractors working at the organisation rather than an integrated organisation.

A well-known consultancy bureau struggled with exactly these same difficulties. They described their question and the symptoms of the problem as: *"How do we regain the strength of the company? We are losing our dignity and our special customers from the old days. The present customers we are attracting are much more 'run-of-the-mill'. What do we all think about this?"*. The mass of management structures, functions that were unclear – from the board of directors to the legal structure of the company (a partnership) - was calling out for a clear structure to be put in place. What struck me most was that the customers were taking over control of the company. Gradually they were starting to determine in which direction the company should be going. From the outside it might have looked as though this change was market-driven, but it was, in fact, a movement of 'following'. The company was following the customers, who were appearing and the company was being forced to sail very much in a zig-zag sort of way. This was not coming from a position of strength or vision but only because the structure and sense of order within the company had become loosened.

Last, but not least, putting things in order, systemically speaking, is important because, when this is done, a company can become more decisive. Being decisive is not just a skill held personally, or by a team within an organisation, but it is more a condition that someone or an organisation can exist in. When you start to notice that it is difficult to come to decisions in your work or that the whole organisation lacks a certain decisiveness, it always pays to check to see if there might be some hidden factors or clients that are getting mixed up in the systemic order of the organisation. The right sort of decisiveness allows an organisation to be outer-directed, and to stay in touch with reality when deciding what to do or not do.

In organisations that are growing it can be a challenge to look after what is new, while at the same time honouring what has come before. Whatever elements in an organisation were there first have priority over those that come in at a later date. If, for example, long-time employees are under-valued, because newer employees are given the important jobs, then an organisation may lose its ability to keep on growing. New employees are then becoming a threat to the whole organisation. On the other hand, when a new team is set up, or a new department or a daughter company is created, there will be an appropriate amount of time when this new element is given priority. This will tend to turn out well if such a new team or department in an organisation can benefit from all that good that is already present in the organisation, as well as being given the freedom to creatively develop into something new too.

11.2 The balance between give and take

This is an important issue for every person in an organisation. Make sure that everyone is able to use their muscle-power, creativity, speciality and other talents to the full. Generally speaking people are able to put their talents to good use if they have the feeling that what they are contributing, is being re-paid, in some way, by the organisation itself. Preferably the compensation they receive is just slightly more than what they have given. Then the exchange between these two elements of the system can flourish and grow.

This principle makes it important that all those involved, employees from within the organisation, as well as customers, and suppliers from outside the organisation, all feel themselves as being seen. The Level of participation and contribution an employee can make to an organisation may also dry up when he or she is not seen enough within an organisation and not recognised.

The principle of the balance of give and take is also valid for organisations as a whole. For companies, and profit organisations, it is clear how the balance of give and take works, because the company or organisation is directly in contact with its customers and as such can always have a direct sense of the inter-change that is happening between the various parties involved.

The sugar company

The owner of a sugar company, that was emitting pollutants into the environment, looked at the people in the areas surrounding his factory and said: *"We know we are a great nuisance for you all, and we know this has a price-tag on for you, even for some of you it is costing you your health.*

Many of you are also working for our company and we appreciate this very much. Although we are constantly working to improve the situation, we realize we cannot compensate for all the trouble we are causing you all. So we are offering you a sports facility and swimming pool". In this situation the local people are seen and feel they are being seen, and such a gesture is a contribution to the social interaction between the factory and its environment. But if the owners of the factory are focussed mainly on profit, and have their eyes fixed on more turnover and growth, they will try to bribe the local people with a sports hall and swimming pool. The local people would feel this immediately. In this case they would not really be seen and will feel they are being used to appease the conscience of the owner. It would end up with the local people not really cooperating with the expansion of the business and the employees who work there would not be able to give their best in the work they would be doing at the factory.

So, whenever we are involved with the balance between give and take there are two matters that are important to consider: acknowledging that there is a debt, and settling the debt. To pass on a raise in salary without, at the same time, acknowledging that this raise is the appropriate reward for work provided, or, as another example, to pay out compensation without at the same time acknowledging that there have been damages done, will not create the right balance. Similarly recognition alone is also not sufficient. Only when the two are combined – recognition plus compensation or reward – can the balance between give and take be right and something new can appear in the future.

With municipalities, schools and many other subsidised institutions, it is possible that sometimes one side of the balance, i.e. where the money actually comes from, gets left out of the picture.

There is a focus and awareness when it comes to delivering services and who should benefit from these services – patients, residents, pupils and so forth – but there may not be so much of a focus on where the money comes from to make all this possible. As an organisational consultant it was amusing for me to see in those days how, in many water management boards the employees of the water management board would know the amount of the 'assessment' for their water board. The 'assessment' is the amount of money that each resident would need to pay to the water board, depending on the surface area of the property they owned. These assessments are the total costs incurred by the water board, divided by the number of residents. Each year a list would be produced on which would be shown exactly how much each water board's assessment had been for that year. For the employees it was always a great honour when the assessment was a low as possible. This meant that for water boards, anything that was not absolutely essential was considered to be nonsense. Their principle was: invest only in what is really needed. Management training, in their eyes, was money completely poured down the drain.

Now I've got a different view and appreciation for the absolute focus that these water boards had on their yearly assessments. These employees were in contact with both sides of the balance of give and take. This meant that they worked hard and always kept an eye on why they were doing what they were doing and for whom they were doing it. In organisations that are subsidised you might ask: to what extent are the employees kept in the picture about how the money flows through the organisation. If money comes into an organisation too easily, and an organisation is not able to compensate by offering the right level of services for this money, the organisation might become sloppy. Subsidy management, to me, seems to be a very special skill.

11.3 Everyone has equal rights to a place in the system.

Society changes. Normally speaking founders of an organisation are just glad that the organisation, that they left behind to be carried on by their successors, continues to do well and the organisation can keep up with the changes in society. When founders of an organisation are honoured as the founders they can stay very much in the background and become a positive and benign force within the whole organisation, while the organisation itself gets on with working for the future. Being honoured in this way, founders are not going to stand in the way of something new happening, but will be supporting it instead.

This general principle, of being recognised and honoured, holds true for all important persons and elements in the history of any organisation. This can be anything from people who did something significant to the structure of an organisation (such as saving a failing business), to elements regarding the actual content of an organisation such as a vision, social ideal or company style. It also is valid for 'those who fell' – those people who have paid a high price in order that the organisation might now be doing well. Whenever these people or elements are excluded in some way from the system of an organisation they start to fester, and grow like cancerous cells under the skin of the organisation. If, however, all the significant people in an organisation have a rightful place in the history of that organisation, then they themselves make it possible for those employees, currently working in that organisation, to feel connected to the very roots of the organisation. This makes a huge contribution to the possibility that everyone in the organisation can find their rightful place both in the stream of history of the organisation, as in the present structure of the organisation. It also allow them to pass on what is appropriate according to the talents and goals of the organisation.

It is true for each employee in an organisation that he or she has a right to be part of that organisation. In that sense there is absolutely no difference, in any particular organisation, between a member of the board of directors of the organisation and a cleaner. If this right to be part of an organisation becomes difficult to maintain, for reasons such as lack of appropriate recognition or validation, or by bullying, or being excluded in other ways, then energy may start to drain out of the organisation. What most essentially contributes to the health and well-being of the people, or, indeed, all elements in an organisation, are such things as: having a place in an organisation, being in touch with the organisation's goals, having a constant exchange of give and take and being recognised and seen. These systemic principles, working together, form a field that supports people and to which they can make a contribution.

Literature

Weber, Gunthard et al
Praxis der Organisationsaufstellung
Carl Auer Systeme Verlag, Heidelberg, Germany
ISBN 3-89670-117-7
Accessible book with articles, originating from a conference in 1998 on business constellations in Germany. Contributions from most of the renowned pioneers in this field. German

Grochowiak, Klaus & Castella
Systemdynamische Organisationsberatung
Carl Auer Systeme Verlag, Heidelberg, Germany
ISBN 3-89670-180-0
Practical and very clear book, both with theoretical fundamentals and practical examples. German

Sparrer, Insa & Matthias Varga von Kibéd
Ganz im Gegenteil. Tetralemmaarbeit und andere Grundformen Systemischer Strukturaufstellungen
Carl Auer-Systeme Verlag, Heidelberg, Germany
ISBN 3-89670-121-5
This book is an introduction to structural constellations, developed by Insa Sparrer and Matthias Varga von Kibéd. Structural constellations focus more on the structure of an business issue or problem than on the content of the issue. For that reason structure constellations are very applicable in the business context. German.

Stam, Jan Jacob
Bringing the roots of organizations to light
Uitgeverij Het Noorderlicht

About the author

Jan Jacob Stam (1954) came in touch with family constellations while working as an organisation consultant. He immediately had the idea that this method could also be used to look at questions coming up in the organisations with which he was working. He took several training courses in Germany, founded the Bert Hellinger Institute Nederland, together with his wife Bibi Schreuder in 2000, and two years later opened the publishing house Het Noorderlicht (The Northern Light). Jan Jacob Stam is continually exploring new ways of deepening systemic work and the possibilities for its application. *"What I encounter there gives so many new insights about how systems work, and about organisations and society as a whole. But I also feel very humble about all of this. I really enjoy sharing the insights that come up, in workshops, in exchanges with colleagues through doing trainings and in this book".*

Jan Jacob Stam

Middelberterweg 48
9723 EW Groningen
The Netherlands

info@hellingerinstituut.nl
www.hellingerinstituut.nl

About the Dutch Bert Hellinger Institute

The Bert Hellinger Institute the Netherlands (BHIN) was founded by Jan Jacob Stam and Bibi Schreuder in 2000 and since 2015, Barbara Hoogenboom is co-owner.

Bert Hellinger encouraged Jan Jacob to take this step and allowed him to use his name. To this day, we are in regular contact and exchange with Bert Hellinger, now 91 years old.

What characterizes BHIN is:

- On the one hand, the loyalty to the foundation of the systemic phenomenological work the way Bert Hellinger discovered and described it. Working with the consciences, the principles (workings) and the patterns that arise;

- On the other hand, the continuing, phenomenological, openness to what wants to develop and reveal itself. This means for example, that we look at this work and the role of facilitator in constellations in a different way than in 2000. And that we have said our farewell to habits and interventions that were previously customary.

We can imagine, and even encourage the participants in our courses, to incorporate systemic work in their 'own toolkit' with their other 'tools'. That they develop their own style and mix. But with the implicit assumption that people are clear in their communication about their mixture.

This is only possible, if at BHIN we stay, as purely and precisely as possible, close to the foundations or the phenomenological work. That is what we enjoy most, and with a lot of love. Ánd that is what we want people to recognise us for, both meanings of the word, in the outside world.

More information and contact:
info@hellingerinstituut.nl
www.hellingerinstituut.nl

About Systemic Books

Systemic Books is an international independent Publishing House focused on creating high quality content selected from the broad range of books available. The books range from classic to cutting edge work with new adaptations of the systemic school of thought and working. This way, Systemic Books aims to answer to the different levels of knowledge people have or need on systemic work.

Systemic Books wass founded in joint energy by Siets Bakker and Barbara Piper in 2016. When they met in 2015, their knowledge of and interest in the systemic perspective and their shared love for books, planted the seed for Systemic Books. This initiative combines their knowledge in the publishing world and efforts to make systemic work available to a global audience. We translate, edit and publish books. Great books about the systemic school of thought. We make use of all modern possibilities in publishing and printing to make these books available all over the world.

More information and contact:
contact@systemicbooks.com
www.systemicbooks.com